PITCH PERFECT

PITCH PERFECT

HOW TO SAY IT RIGHT THE FIRST TIME, EVERY TIME

BILL McGOWAN
AND ALISA BOWMAN

HARPER
BUSINESS

An Imprint of HarperCollins*Publishers*
www.harpercollins.com

HarperCollins books may be purchased for educational, business,
or sales promotional use. For information, please e-mail the
Special Markets Department at SPsales@harpercollins.com.

FIRST EDITION

Designed by Jo Anne Metsch

Illustrations by dix! Digital Prepress Inc.

Library of Congress Cataloging-in-Publication Data has been applied for.

ISBN 978-0-06-227322-2

14 15 16 17 18   OV/RRD   10 9 8 7 6 5 4 3 2 1

To Donna, Andrew, Kara, and Paulina,
all masters at communicating
what matters most.

CONTENTS

ACKNOWLEDGMENTS

*P*ITCH PERFECT WOULD not have happened without the generous support of many people. First, my thanks go to Alisa Bowman, my coauthor, for suggesting this collaboration several years ago, after I had coached her for a media tour for her own book. Alisa masterfully translated the tenets of our media-training sessions into the framework you see in this book and gave the project life. If it were not for Alisa, I would surely still be staring at a blank screen. Creative, smart, kind, diligent, and patient, she is everything anyone would want in a teammate.

A special thanks to Hollis Heimbouch at HarperCollins, who exhibited unbound enthusiasm for this project from our very first meeting. Her warmth, encouragement, and expert guidance made the writing process a delight. Validation that this book was distinctive and merited publishing came from my longtime friend and agent Wayne Kabak of WSK Management. To have a man of talent, wisdom, and integrity like Wayne in your corner is invaluable.

Writing this book while keeping my day job was possible thanks only to the hard work and professionalism of the entire team at Clarity Media Group. Lucy Cherkasets took control of running many aspects of the business with such skill that I have no intention of taking them back. My assistant, Mariko Takahashi, kept my chaotic schedule under control and freed up sufficient mental bandwidth for me to focus on writing. And Tiffany Sanchez was an eager sampler of random chapters, always providing encouragement that I was on the right track.

The willingness of our other Clarity coaches to shoulder a heavier workload was crucial to the book's completion. Melissa Hellen stepped up big-time and delivered her usual excellence, as did Bill Cassara, Marisa Thomas, Ken Fuhr, Jim Paymar, Jennifer Fukui, Dylan Chalfy, John Johnston, and Janet Carlson.

The experiences I drew upon from thousands of training sessions were a result of the kindness and generosity of those who helped grow our business over the past thirteen years. The following, in alphabetical order, have transcended the status of client and are regarded at Clarity as business-building benefactors: Roger Ailes, Howard Arenstein, Laura Arrillaga-Andreessen, Brandee Barker, Wajma Basharyar, Emi Battaglia, Winnie Beatty, Mike Bertolino, Gurdon Blackwell, Julia Boorstin, Jacques Brand, Adam Bryant, Jerry Buckley, Rebecca Caruso, Sean Cassidy, Nathan Christopher, Lou Cona, Jocelyn Cordova, Karen DiSanto, Jeannine Dowling, Pat Eisemann, Daniel Ek, Sheila Feren-Thurston, Debbie Frost, Lisa Green, Carol Giardino, Maire Griffin, Judy Grossman, Carisa Hays, Susan Henderson, HL Group, Kristen Jones-Connell, Alexander Jutkowitz, Claire Kaye, Thomas Keller, Scott Lahde, Neal Lenarsky, Mary Lengle, Santina Leuci, Linda Lipman, Derek Mains, Juli Mandel-Sloves, Eli Manning, Caryn Marooney, Wynton Marsalis, Mike Mayzel, Zsoka McDonald, Diane McNulty, Dana Bowne Metz, Katie Burke Mitic, Denise Morrison, Elena Nachmanoff, Jessica O'Callaghan, Tanya Pushkine, David Rhodes, Stephanie Ruhle, Sheryl Sandberg, Ruchi Sanghvi, Anthony Sanzio, Elliot Schrage, Amanda Schumacher, Nell Scovell, Pam Snook, Cara Stein, Jonny Thaw, Pamela Thomas-Graham, Matt Traub,

Karyn Twaronite, Judy Twersky, Jane Ubell-Meyer, Loretta Ucelli, Jonathan Wald, Carolyn Wall, Angela Watts, Kate White, Meghan Womack, and Eileen Wu.

I've learned the art of storytelling at the knee of so many talented people over the years, but two superstars stand out. Michael Rubin, whom I describe in chapter 4, has brilliant insights into how stories should unfold. I was lucky enough to be one of his many protégés. Peter Brennan, the creative genius behind *A Current Affair*, is in a league of his own when it comes to knowing what elements of a story are crucial and conveying them dramatically and efficiently.

While incredibly fortunate to have the friendship and support of these wonderful people, I am positively blessed that the most gifted writer I know and the most insightful copy editor around just also happens to be the love of my life, my wife, Donna Cornachio. To closely read every word of the manuscript with a keenly analytical and discerning eye (and a much-needed red pencil) is surely a sign of true love. Her encouragement and inspiration made this happen.

PITCH PERFECT

INTRODUCTION

Speak little, do much.
—Benjamin Franklin

I F JUST ONE piece of advice from this book brings you career success, don't thank me. Track down a guy named Roy Schwasinger and thank him. You'll find him in a federal prison somewhere.

I met Schwasinger thirty years ago when I was working as a correspondent for *A Current Affair*, the tabloid newsmagazine TV program that ran from 1986 to 1996. Schwasinger was your stereotypical bad guy. Because of the silent *ch*, his name nearly rhymed with *swastika*, further contributing to his aura of villainy. As an antigovernment activist, he was a real boil on the backside of all public and elected officials. He filed false liens, subpoenas, and arrest warrants against certain judges and prosecutors in an elaborate scheme to make their lives miserable. Even worse, he was accused of running a scam on destitute American farmers, falsely promising them, through his sham organization We the People, that he would help them win back their foreclosed farms for a mere $300 court-filing fee. That's right, you guessed it. The cash was going straight into Schwasinger's grubby pocket.

To imagine Schwasinger, think of the Great Santini on a bad acid trip. He was of medium height, a stocky man in his fifties sporting a military-style crew cut and a wardrobe straight off the rack at Sears. The permanent scowl on his face conveyed an unambiguous message: get away from me or I'll hurt you. He turned down all media requests for interviews and made himself about as scarce as a survivalist in rural Idaho.

One thing was sure: If I could get close enough to ask him some tough questions, it would make for some great TV. Little did I know just how great that footage would be.

Schwasinger ignored my requests for sit-down interviews, so I flew to Fort Collins, Colorado, met up with the camera crew, drove to Schwasinger's house, and waited for him to emerge. Walking up and knocking on the door might seem to you like a logical course of action, but that's actually the last thing reporters generally do. Standing on his stoop would have allowed Schwasinger to call the police and claim that we were trespassing. It also would have tipped him off to our presence, possibly causing him to stay behind locked doors and wait until we lost interest and left town.

No, we wanted to wait until he left the house and put himself in some unprotected public place. Then we would catch him by surprise. So inside our rented Ford Explorer we sat. One hour ticked by. Then two. Then three. Then five. Then ten. This was the predigital era, long before Facebook, smartphone apps, and other distractions. Thoroughly exploring and analyzing all the current office gossip used up only about two hours. After that, the boredom-killing got more challenging. The fact that Hollywood filmmakers can make stakeouts appear glamorous is a true testament to their creative genius.

Finally, at ten the following morning, Roy emerged. We patiently watched as he got into his stinkin' Lincoln and drove off. After hours of mind-numbing inactivity, I suddenly got this surge of adrenaline that caused nearly every nerve ending in my body to tingle. I even forgot how badly I had to pee.

We followed at a safe distance of several car lengths for a mile or so, until our black hat in the story pulled into a parking space outside the Larimer County Courthouse. We parked five spaces away.

"You guys get the camera ready to roll while I go up and make nice," I said to my crew. "Just make sure you walk up rolling."

In television parlance, this is what's called an ambush or a sandbagging: walk up, cameras rolling, and as Andy Cohen says, "watch what happens live." Under normal circumstances, cornered animals like Schwasinger don't stay composed, and of course that's what we were counting on.

"Mr. Schwasinger. . . . I'm Bill McGowan from *A Current Affair*," I said, trying to keep my surging adrenaline from making me sound nervous. "I'd like to ask you some questions about We the People. . . ."

Out of the corner of my eye, I could see our cameraman to my side. I gave a quick look to make sure the red tally light on the front of the camera was lit. Yes, he was recording. Good.

The minute Schwasinger noticed the camera, he cut short our handshake. His eyes ferociously darted around as they sized up the severity of this pop-up crisis. If a thought bubble had appeared over his head, it would have read, *WTF is going on here?*

"I cannot answer anything," he said.

"Why can you not answer anything?" I pressed.

We were nose-to-nose. "Because I'm under a restraining order from disclosing anything. Go to the U.S. District Court in the District of Nebraska and you'll find it," he said, his saliva spray hitting me in the face, a disgusting development I was able to overlook because I knew I had this fish hooked.

I had checked with the prosecutor earlier. As a result, I already knew there were no restrictions on Schwasinger talking. In fact, the prosecutor predicted that Schwasinger would tell me that lie about the restraining order.

"Right, we have, sir, and we want to know why you're taking farmers' money!"

His goon-in-tow tried to stick his hand in the lens of our camera as Roy walked away, a cliché gesture that, to an audience, says, "bad guy trying to take cover."

As Schwasinger tried to flee, I managed to keep up with him, walking alongside him, step for step, pressing him for an answer as the cameras followed. After about seven or eight steps, Roy gave me pure TV gold. He reared back and threw a formidable right cross that connected solidly with my chin and throat. His fist connected close to my wireless microphone, so it gave the audio of the punch an overly dramatic, bone-crunching quality.

My head snapped back and I stumbled, but strangely I felt no pain. In fact, I bounced right back up like an inflatable shmoo doll.

My first thought? *Whatever happens after this is gravy! The office is going to* love *this footage!*

My next thought? *Isn't that guy over there a cop?* Indeed he was. We showed the videotape of the punch to the Fort Collins policeman, and he promptly handcuffed and arrested my attacker.

It was later that day, during a precautionary visit to the hospital, that I had an epiphany. My jaw might have been sore, but my eyes had suddenly been opened. There must be countless other people (not so nefarious, one hopes) who handle all kinds of public communication situations poorly. If Roy Schwasinger had received some good advice, he could have tried to persuade me instead of trying to deck me. There were at least a half dozen communication tricks he could have used to emerge from our ambush with his dignity and image intact. After all, when you coldcock a reporter in front of rolling cameras, your stature in the community tends to suffer.

In the aftermath of the "farm belt," as it came to be known around the office, I suddenly noticed example after example of someone doing and saying something stupid during a high-stakes situation. It was a lot like looking up the meaning of an unfamiliar word and then suddenly noticing that same word in three different places that same week. These communication self-saboteurs weren't just people like Schwasinger who found themselves sand-bagged by a reporter. They were celebrities and politicians and executives and everyone in between.

Long before Sarah Palin provided us with endless amusement, former vice president Dan Quayle was almost single-handedly validating the need for communication coaches. For years he was the benchmark for bonehead statements. Who can forget his attempt to paraphrase the United Negro College Fund's slogan, "A mind is a terrible thing to waste?" which instead came out as, "What a waste it is to lose one's mind. Or not to have a mind is being very wasteful. How true that is." The degree of his wastefulness was hard to dispute.

But plenty of household names were keeping the veep company.

The word *genius* isn't applicable in football. A genius is a guy like Norman Einstein.

—*Joe Theismann, NFL football quarterback and sports analyst*

Smoking can kill you. And if you've been killed, you've lost a very important part of your life.

—*Brooke Shields, model and actress*

Outside of the killings, DC has one of the lowest crime rates in the country.   —*Mayor Marion Barry, Washington, DC*

Pick an era, any era, and you'll find faux pas of historic proportions. Many of these memorable manglings came from people who belonged to the communication One Percent Club. They were the elite public speakers—politicians, athletes, actresses, and executives in the public eye. These were folks who had a team of image experts and communications specialists at the ready. So that got me thinking: If *they* say things off pitch, what chance do the rest of us, the ninety-nine percenters, have of tiptoeing through the communications minefield unscathed? Someone capable of steering them in the right direction and building sound communication instincts could really make a positive impact and be a valuable resource.

It would be a few more years before I realized that maybe I could be the one providing that trusted counsel.

At the time, I was writing and producing long-format news magazine stories for Connie Chung at ABC News's *20/20*, a position that would soon be coming to an end. I like Connie a lot. She is warm and gracious, with a deliciously edgy sense of humor that strays into bluntly provocative territory every now and then. But *20/20* was a no-win situation for both of us. Connie was in the unenviable and frustrating position of being pushed to the periphery of significance. As her producer, I could clearly see the future. ABC was a dead end for Connie. As a result, planning my own escape was a must.

It was around this time that a friend asked me if I was interested in producing a three-minute branding video for a client of hers who was launching a job-search website. She wanted a substantive sizzle reel to prove to the venture-capital community that her company was worthy of funding.

Part of the shoot involved a sit-down interview. After it was over, she asked, "Do you mind playing some of the videotape back so I can see how I did?" Initially I thought what a pain this was going to be, setting up a special monitor and cutting into valuable shooting time for a sneak preview just to satisfy her curiosity. But I had just crossed the threshold from TV journalist to businessman, where pleasing the client at all costs is the prime directive. So of course my response was "Sure, we can do that." And it was during that playback that my transformational "aha" moment occurred. Instinctively I started telling this client that she would be better served starting her answers a different way, keeping her answers in an affirmative tone and active, rather than passive voice. "Oh and while you're at it, sit forward in your chair a bit, don't be afraid to punctuate your key points with some hand gestures and maintain more sustained eye contact with your interviewer."

She reached forward to hit PAUSE on the video player and said, "This is what you should be doing. I mean I'm sure you're a perfectly good TV producer, but you're *really* good at this. Do you have any idea of the value of this kind of guidance?"

The friend who had connected us overheard this conversation and must have tucked it away because, at a cocktail party the following week, when the head of PR for *Real Simple* magazine said to her, "We just had to get rid of our media trainer. Do you know a good one?" she said, "I sure do." So in a somewhat intimidating, initiation-by-fire situation, my first client was one of the hottest magazines on the newsstands.

The new emboldened me went back to Connie to tell her that it was time for me to move on. The next chapter in my career was about to start.

Now, after twelve years as a communications coach, I study language just as meticulously as the former *New York Times* statistician Nate Silver studies numbers. Watching a big interview or major speech on TV with me is probably as annoying as going to a movie with a film director: I just can't help dissecting, analyzing, and critiquing. Anyone who monitors their Facebook Newsfeed during a political convention, a presidential debate, or the Academy Awards is probably tempted to defriend me.

On any given day, I help my clients decide what to say and how to say it. That may include coaching:

- Corporate executives to craft a compelling and relatable narrative that stresses the possibilities of what lies ahead more than any current problems.
- Heads of nonprofits to bring a sense of poignancy and urgency to their case for why their cause is deserving of people's support.
- Employees to stand out by articulating their thoughts with clarity, brevity, and conviction.
- Public speakers, not only to overcome their nerves and deliver

their content without stumbles, but also keep the audience's attention throughout their speech or presentation and ultimately say something memorable.

- Authors to talk about their work in a way that fuels book sales but without sounding overtly salesy.
- Professional on-air reporters and anchors not to become a caricature of a TV news talking head.
- Computer engineers at technology companies to convey clearly the practical importance of what they've designed and built.
- Sales teams to win over new clients by telling a compelling story about their company's distinctiveness.
- Job seekers to highlight their competitive strengths by illustrating them through case-study-type storytelling.

No matter the client or the scenario and regardless of whether I'm working with people one-on-one or in groups, I'm often asked for advice about the same areas of concern. Broadly (notice I did not say "from a macro perspective"?—you'll learn more about breaking free of mindless corporate jargon in chapter 7), that could be:

- How do I project greater confidence and command?
- How can I admit to a mistake without losing people's confidence?
- How do I inspire others to deliver their very best?
- How do I ask for what I deserve in a way that's persuasive, not whiny?

The more specific guidance often centers on:

- What do I do with my hands while I'm talking?
- How do I get rid of filler words (*ums* and *ahs*)?
- How do I bring more gravitas to the sound of my voice?
- How can I be more concise and stop rambling?

No matter the concern, the solutions reside in the Seven Principles of Persuasion that you'll learn more about throughout the pages of *Pitch Perfect*. I leaned on these principles during my broadcast career and have since adapted and developed them to help anyone communicate more effectively in virtually any situation. They apply to everything you could possibly ever want to say at work and even at home.

It gives me great personal satisfaction to teach some of the principles to family and friends who ask for help with a wedding toast, winning answers for a big job interview, or techniques for delivering a great bar mitzvah speech. I've also had the privilege of coaching some people who are regarded by others as naturals, the Roy Hobbses of communications. What I've learned is that those born-great types are rare. The overwhelming majority of people we admire for their public speaking prowess have two simple ingredients behind their greatness:

1. They put themselves in the hands of an insightful coach who isn't trying to turn them into somebody else but rather brings out their best.
2. Once they have useful guidance, they work tirelessly to get better.

I'll make a deal with you. This book will take care of number one. I will impart everything I know, everything I have learned during my four thousand coaching sessions. What you will come away with is a thorough yet simple set of principles for deftly handling a wide variety of personal and professional communication scenarios so you can achieve the best of all possible results. And if you have a few good laughs along the way, just consider it an added bonus.

Number two is on you. Prepare, prepare, prepare. Practice, practice, practice. From here on, accept every invitation you get to do public speaking. Be the first one with your hand in the air when someone asks, "Would anybody like to say a few words?" Think of me as your golf or tennis coach. I'll give you the secret to the right swing, but then you have to go out and play so you can ingrain this new muscle memory.

Let's each hold up our respective ends of the bargain. That's the best way I know for you to become Pitch Perfect.

1

THE LANGUAGE OF SUCCESS

Think twice before you speak, because your words and influence will plant the seed of either success or failure in the mind of your listener.

—NAPOLEON HILL

IF ELOQUENCE WERE a commodity listed on the New York Stock Exchange, every analyst on Wall Street would issue a buy order. That's because its value constantly rises, and investment in it pays increasingly huge dividends.

At no time was this more apparent to me than the afternoon an executive at a major company asked me to improve the communication skills of one of his managers. "Donald is not going to advance in the organization if his presentation skills don't improve," I was told. At first I was stunned. Did communication skills matter that much that a manager could not advance without them? In this company, they did. The good news was, Donald's issues were common and fixable. His delivery had lacked any sense that he found his own content even mildly interesting, and rather than stories, he relied on empty industry jargon that ensured his presentation would be forgettable. I'm happy to say that six months after our sessions together, Donald joined the VP ranks at his company and has outlasted many of his peers.

Since then, however, I've heard about the importance of com-

munication skills from so many executives that I'm no longer surprised.

From clients I also hear:

"I have good ideas, but I just can't seem to convey them well to
my bosses in meetings."

"Landing this big account probably hinges on this one presentation."

"I get called back for second- and third-round interviews but I
never seem to get the big job."

And that's just in the workplace. Think of all the personal scenarios in which we're judged by not just what we do but what we
say: first dates, college interviews, meeting future in-laws, delicate
family conversations, and resolving conflicts with close friends.

Whether at work or at home, great communication skills are
your secret to holding someone's attention, making a persuasive
point, being remembered, and appearing smart and confident.
Every time you speak, it's an opportunity to inform, influence,
and inspire. The right language—both verbal and nonverbal—
can make you seem self-assured, persuasive, and certain. It can
move people, changing their minds and emotions. It can stir them
to listen closely to your every word and remember you long after
you've left the room.

THE PITCH-PERFECT MOMENT

During pivotal moments of our lives, results are often determined
not by what we do, but instead by what we say.

Saying the right thing the right way can make the difference
between sealing the deal or losing the account, advancing in your

career or stagnating, earning a powerful ally or burning an important career bridge. Get it right and your reputation will shine from that halo effect awarded to those who are seen as confident, smart, likable, and sincere. Get it wrong and you run the risk of being labeled annoying, tedious, ineffectual, or irrelevant.

During such moments, it's important to be Pitch Perfect, to use precisely the right tone to convey the right message to the right person at the right time. Such Pitch-Perfect moments serve as crucial junctures in our personal and professional lives. In business they take place every day, sometimes several times a day. They come up during meetings, presentations, events, parties, in hallways, over coffee, on smartphones, and in front of cameras.

One of my own most memorable Pitch-Perfect moments unfolded in a taxicab speeding south on the 101 just outside of San Francisco.

I had just scored Facebook, my biggest client in the eight years since I launched my communications-coaching firm. I flew in the night before and stayed at the Westin on the recommendation of Brandee Barker, Facebook's director of communications. Brandee suggested the hotel because, as she put it, "It's practically within walking distance of the Facebook offices at 1601 California Avenue."

The training day was scheduled to start at 9:00 a.m., so, driven by my business mantra that "if you're on time, you're late," I sauntered down to the hotel lobby at 7:45 a.m. and approached the concierge for a play-it-safe double check.

"1601 California—that's walking distance, right?"

"Well, . . ." he said, with an expression that conveyed, *If you're a total nutcase I guess you could walk it.* "Probably better to take a cab. Walking it would probably take you forty-five minutes."

I ignored this first-stage crisis warning. *Hmm,* I thought. *Maybe Brandee's a really fast walker.* Into the cab I got.

The stage-two crisis warning came ten minutes later, when the cabbie was having trouble finding 1601 California.

Stage-three alarms sounded when 1601 California turned out to not be Facebook headquarters, but rather a nail salon. During meltdown moments like this, it's amazing how tightly a person can find himself in the grip of denial. As the cab pulled away, I looked toward the second floor of the modest building praying that somehow the biggest social network in the world was headquartered above Mani/Pedi-land.

It wasn't.

At 8:20 a.m., a text from my assistant back in New York came through: "Facebook is on the phone and they want to know where you are."

More denial washed over me. *Maybe I just got the building number mixed up,* I thought.

I called and got Brandee's assistant. "Hi, it's Bill McGowan. I'm standing in front of 1601 California, but I can't seem to find the office."

"OK, well describe what you see in front of you."

(This was before Facebook developed the location-based Check-In feature, which would have immediately exposed the severity of my screw-up.)

"Well, let's see. There's a bagel shop to my right, a dry cleaners to my left . . ."

"What city are you in?"

"I'm in San Francisco."

"We're located in Palo Alto!"

"Oh." I didn't want to create the awkward silence that ensued, but my hard swallow took a good two seconds. "About how long would it take me to get there from here?"

"In morning rush-hour traffic? About an hour."

I mentioned possibly renting a car or hailing a cab. The assistant replied, "Well, whatever you do, do it fast because Brandee is *livid!*"

Unfortunately for me, Brandee had not planned to start me out slowly. My 9:00 a.m. meeting was scheduled with Facebook's COO,

Sheryl Sandberg. My 10:30? CEO Mark Zuckerberg. This was a bad day to be late.

As the taxi weaved its way out of downtown San Francisco, I gazed enviously at street sweepers and restaurant delivery guys. How badly I wanted to switch places with them and not be dealing with this Silicon Valley implosion. That confidence-killing voice on my shoulder was now screaming, "There's no way you're going to be able to recover from this fiasco." For more than a fleeting moment, I considered telling the cabbie to just take me straight to the airport. My grand plan to break into the tech sector, a plan that had been two to three years in the making, was now looking dead on my nonarrival.

Then it came to me. It was time to heed my own advice. If there was ever a time to be Pitch Perfect, now was that time.

Just own up to the fact that you screwed up, I told myself. *Owning up to mistakes is something that is in increasingly short supply these days.*

I pulled out my iPhone and began carefully constructing a text to Brandee, "Thoroughly inexcusable. Absolutely horrible way to start off this working relationship. It's all on me. I'm sorry."

I knew that the beauty of offering an unequivocal expression of regret was that I could then pivot from being back on my heels to going on the offensive again. I continued, "All I can tell you is, once I get there, we are going to have an amazing day."

Within seconds, she texted back, "You're right. This is terrible. It's not only a terrible reflection on you, but it's a bad reflection on me since I'm the one responsible for bringing you in."

I was glad Brandee was venting via text. The more we could address this toxicity now, the faster we would be able to change the dynamic for the better.

That morning, 101 was not only the number of the highway we took, but I believe the taxi's speedometer flirted in those triple digits a couple of times. Even at that speed, the rate of our progress seemed only slightly better than downloading a full-length movie

with a dial-up connection. Would the cab ever drop me at the correct 1601 California Avenue in Palo Alto?

When I arrived it was 9:20 a.m. To my relief and delight, I discovered that Brandee was the picture of professionalism. She offered a gracious welcome and said, "I managed to push Sheryl back
a bit. How much time do you think you'll need to set up your video
equipment?"

My normal thirty-minute setup was done in ten, and the sessions went extremely well, so well that Sheryl asked if she could
swing back at the end of the day for some extra time.

Of course I agreed.

That was four years ago. Delightfully, I've been a fixture at Facebook ever since, working with some of the smartest, kindest, and
most creative people I've ever met. Communicating poorly would
not just have created tension, it would have lost me the client. I had
to get it right the first time. There was not going to be an opportunity for a communication do-over.

Thinking back on our lives, I'm sure we can all remember a
few Pitch-Perfect moments. Maybe we muddled through the experience and managed to somehow get it right. Or maybe things
didn't go so well. Rather than wow someone, we underwhelmed.

We were not Pitch Perfect. Rather, we were Pitch Poor, and
whenever we think about that experience, we cringe, because
there's no take two.

Many people look back on Pitch-Poor performances with a mix-
ture of regret (*I wish I had said it differently*) and relief (*thank goodness
that's over*). The thing is: it's not over. Sure, that one Pitch-Perfect
opportunity has passed, but many, many more opportunities lie
ahead. We tend to think that such high-stakes situations are rare,
that these important moments take place only when giving a presentation in front of your boss or resolving a terrible argument
with someone very close to us. In reality, it has been estimated that
we spend 70 to 80 percent of our waking hours in some form of
communication. During many of those hours, we absolutely need

to say it right. Pitch-Perfect moments take place every day, maybe even several times a day, when we're:

- Chatting up the boss at the office party.
- Pitching a new client.
- Closing a deal.
- Speaking up during the weekly office meeting.
- Making small talk with clients, coworkers, and supervisors.
- Dealing with tense situations.
- Breaking bad news.
- Apologizing for mistakes.
- Congratulating colleagues on their successes.
- Asking for raises, new titles, or promotions.

THE SEVEN BENEFITS OF ELOQUENCE

My goal for you in this book is exactly the same as what we accomplish for the clients who hire us. I want you to:

Rise up the Corporate Ladder

Communication skills make you more promotable. When the Center for Talent Innovation conducted a yearlong study of more than 4,000 professionals and 268 senior executives, leadership was an absolute essential to securing top jobs, and leadership was defined as: gravitas (the ability to project confidence), excellent communication skills, and a polished appearance. Among the top blunders that kept people from getting promoted, according to the study: racially biased comments, off-color jokes, crying, swearing, flirting, public scratching, avoiding eye contact, rambling, giggling too much, and speaking shrilly. All of those blunders stem from poor communication skills.

Get the Results You Want

It's been said that two thirds of ideas are rejected not because they are bad but because they were communicated poorly. That translates into a lot of people who have great ideas but can't cash in on them because they can't articulate them.

Make Your Point in Less Time

According to the *Harvard Business Review*, businesses spend less than 2 percent of their time discussing strategic issues. That means that, if you want your idea to stand out, you must present it not only clearly, but also concisely.

Overcome Anxiety

In the annual survey of life's greatest fears, public speaking is perennially wedged between dying (number one) and flying (number three). The techniques in *Pitch Perfect* will help to alleviate prespeech jitters so you can overcome anxiety and instead focus on your performance. Clients tell us that the ultimate watershed moment is when they stop tossing and turning the night before a speech or presentation and graduate to feeling an eager buzz and excitement. Imagine enjoying speaking in front of others and swapping out that pit in your stomach for a real rush of enthusiasm.

Get More Done

People who communicate effectively are flat out more productive. When you say it right the first time, people hear it right the first time you say it, there are fewer questions, less need to explain things again and again, and fewer misunderstandings.

Raise More Money

In my professional life, nothing is more gratifying than the pro bono speech coaching I do for nonprofits. The notion that communicating more effectively to an audience of potential donors can spark more philanthropy and greater resources for people in need all over the world is nothing short of electrifying. From experience I can tell you that putting a Pitch-Perfect framing on your message gets results.

Recently I worked with two inspiring men who lead Many Hopes, a nonprofit that helps impoverished and homeless children in Kenya. I coached them to fine-tune their stories, bring a sense of clarity and urgency to their cause, and remove the stereotypical hard sell behind the request for contributions. The first fund-raiser after the coaching session resulted in five times more contributions than previous events. A subsequent training for their volunteers sparked a 10 percent growth in the effectiveness of fund-raising campaigns over the previous year.

Stop Apologizing So Much

With good communication skills, you can rest assured that you say it best the first time. There's no second-guessing yourself, tripping over your tongue, or accidentally putting your foot in your mouth.

THE SECRETS OF PITCH-PERFECT COMMUNICATORS

When I ask people to name some of the best communicators around, they often mention the late founder of Apple computers, Steve Jobs. Others mention Sheryl Sandberg of Facebook, Jeff Bezos of Amazon, Robin Roberts of *Good Morning America*, or various politicians ranging from Bill Clinton to Ronald Reagan. Anyone who is extremely accomplished at what he or she does makes it look easy, giving rise to the misconception that gifted communicators are the lucky recipients of some great-communicator gene. But that's not true at all. Great communicators are not genetically pre-determined. They are made.

Nearly all of these great communicators have been coached by people like me. They also do the following—all of which you can do as well.

Practice

Most professionals who make their living in front of audiences and cameras would never dream of ad-libbing. It's quite the opposite. They all decide what they want to say long before they say it. According to *Inside Apple*, Steve Jobs practiced dozens of times before a big presentation, staging and rehearsing so that nothing was left to chance.

This doesn't mean that you must practice everything seventy times before you have it Pitch Perfect. Some people need to do it multiple times to ingrain it, while others suffer from being too rehearsed. The point is simply this: don't delude yourself into thinking that you can skip preparation. That is a recipe for disaster. And be careful! The more accomplished you become at public speaking, the more you will be tempted to shortchange your preparation. If you succumb to that urge, you will live to regret it.

The beauty of communication: it's easy to practice. It's not like trying to be a better skier and needing a snow-covered hill, a condition you find three times a year if you are lucky. We usually talk all day long, so the opportunities to try out new strategies and get them Pitch Perfect are plentiful.

Develop Distinctiveness

Can you imagine how boring life would be if we all sounded alike? It's no wonder so many of us find our minds wandering during presentations, lectures, and conference calls. Spoken communication today, especially in the workplace, has a numbing sameness to it. Many of us have adopted a monotonous lexicon of meaningless phrases ("so if you look at this from a marketing perspective, rather than a managerial perspective," blah, blah, blah) that get delivered much the same way. It's understandable, because we learn communication mainly through osmosis. But far too many people mistakenly think that this predictable and boring way of communicating represents a safe comfort zone. In reality, it's nothing more than a conformity zone that denies us the opportunity to develop a personal style that's distinctive and straightforward. Confinement to the conformity zone condemns you to sounding like everybody else and increasing your forgettability factor.

It's easy to think, *Everyone else is doing it, so this must be the commonly acceptable way to do it.* My belief is precisely the opposite: if everyone else is doing it, you don't want to do it at all. To me, spoken communication is like the stock market. When you see too many people all going in one direction, it's time to do the opposite. That's what John D. Rockefeller did in 1928. When a shoeshine boy offered him a stock tip, Rockefeller thought, *If everyone else—including shoeshine boys—are in the market, the market must be overbought.* He got out, investing his wealth elsewhere. When the market crashed a year later, his family fortune didn't crash with it.

I want you to be memorable. The purpose of this book is *not* to have everyone communicating as if they're reading the same script. There's nothing worse than that. The status quo is numbing—it causes listeners to tune out. When it comes to communicating well, you don't want to blend into the crowd. I want you to stand out.

PITCH-PERFECT POINTER

To overcome any reluctance to leave your comfort zone, try this exercise. The next time you are trapped in an audience listening to a boring presenter, pull out a sheet of paper and make two columns. Give one column the header "Fresh and Original," and the other "Hackneyed and Clichéd." Mark everything the speaker does that represents a new and fresh approach in the Original column, and, conversely, everything you've heard a million times in the Clichéd column. I suggest this exercise often to clients. I always tell them to "avoid everyone in your Clichéd column like the plague," but unfortunately, not everyone gets the joke.

Show Crisp Conviction

Good communicators don't equivocate. They don't start sentences with "I think that . . ." They also avoid wishy-washy language, such as *sort of* and *kind of.* They have the courage to say what they mean and confidently state their point.

Keep It Short

More is not more. Researchers at Saint Louis University have found that ten to eighteen minutes is the length of time past which you begin a game of diminishing returns on your listener's attention. Take a guess how long President Obama's 2013 inauguration speech was. That's right: eighteen minutes. Coincidence? I doubt it.

Display Sheer Delight

Even if you need to fake it, you want to exude a palpable enthusiasm for the chance to get up and speak. If your audience is getting the sense that you're loving every minute of the opportunity, they will see your performance through a more favorable lens. Conversely, if you look uptight and nervous, that anxiety will spread to your audience.

WHAT I WON'T TELL YOU TO DO

As a communications coach, I deal with language every day. My work revolves around what to say, what not to say, and what to do or not do as you say it. I help TV personalities, authors, athletes, top corporate executives, musicians, and fashion designers discover the pearls within their own personal and professional narratives. Once the content is in place, then it's all about giving them the tools to deliver it with conviction, enthusiasm, and confidence.

Many of the people I train tell me that I'm not like other communication coaches they've dealt with. I ask, "How so?" I'm amazed by the answers. If you've ever been trained for public speaking, read books about it, or listened to advice from well-meaning friends, you've probably been given some cockamamy advice—none of which you'll find in the pages of *Pitch Perfect*. So the following strategies are not meant to be followed under any circumstances. I share them merely for their comedic value.

Imagine Your Audience in Their Underwear

You hear this advice all the time, and I'm at a loss as to why. It's ridiculous, and unless it was started by a Fruit of the Loom marketing executive, it serves no purpose. Not only does it not work, it's a distraction. It takes your focus away from your message and puts it exactly where you don't want it—on something that has nothing to do with what you showed up to say. A much better strategy: deep yogic breathing. When we get nervous, we forget how to breathe properly. We start taking short, shallow breaths, which deplete our lungs of the air necessary to speak with a stable, confident voice. Improper breathing gives the voice that shaky, breathy sound.

Five minutes before you start speaking, take a long inhale through your nose—hold it for a couple of seconds—and then very slowly exhale through the mouth. This technique will quiet all the distracting noise swirling in your head, slow your racing pulse, replenish your lungs with air, and stabilize your voice. Try it. It works!

Channel Your Inner Dumb Blonde

One afternoon a marketing executive from one of the major beauty brands came into my office to practice her delivery on a series of videos slated for her company's website. I asked her what she remembered from the previous media training she'd had with a different company. "All I remember," she said, "is her telling me I needed to channel my inner dumb blonde." I can't imagine a more offensive piece of advice, especially considering the recipient was, in fact, a blonde.

My translation for this shockingly idiotic advice is: be warm and welcoming in your delivery to the camera and show almost child-like enthusiasm for the value of the product you're talking about.

Imagine You're Talking to a Third Grader

This advice is ubiquitous. Dumb it down, mash it into pabulum, spoon-feed it to the ignorant masses. Never has a more misguided notion existed. If you imagine that you are talking to a third grader, you will sound like you are talking to a third grader. Think about that for a moment. What kind of a tone of voice do you use when you are talking to eight-year-olds? Would that tone of voice be appropriate for a room full of adults?

I'm all in favor of forgoing a twenty-five-cent word when a five-cent word will suffice, but that's very different from talking to your audience like they're numskulls. To avoid an insulting tone of condescension, imagine your audience to be a group of college freshman: smart but not yet possessing worldly knowledge.

Buy Time with the Phrase "That's a Great Question!"

This is the most transparent stall tactic out there today. Why not just say what you really mean, which is, "I need more time to think about what the hell I'm going to say." My advice to clients is never comment on the question. Congratulating your interviewer on the cleverness of their question is downright unctuous. Whenever I was told "That's a great question" during my years as a reporter, I always assumed the interview subject was trying to earn my affection with false flattery.

Never Answer the Question

At one time, people may have been able to get away with this strategy, but times have changed. Audiences are more savvy, and they can spot someone who's been trained like a seal (or a political candidate) to never respond to the actual question. This technique spotlights a slick air of evasiveness. It has become so ingrained that people do it even in the face of the most benign questions. For instance, if you were asked, "So how about this weather, huh? Isn't it beautiful outside?" the normal answer would be "It sure is. It's gorgeous." It would be plain weird to approach that question with a guarded, controlled, overly formal speech about the topic of the weather: "Well if you look at the conditions from a meteorological perspective, what we're seeing is that the metrics for this time of year are somewhat skewed." I wish I could tell you that that example is a ridiculous exaggeration of what I hear on a regular basis, but it's not.

Three quarters of the questions we're asked carry no risk to answering them directly, so to create the feel of a real conversation, take them head-on. The remaining quarter might be leading, snarky, insinuating, or outright accusatory questions. For these, state directly what you want to say about the *topic* of the question rather than answering it directly. This is part of the Draper Principle, and you'll learn more about it in chapter 9.

Say Someone's Name Over and Over

On principle, I never buy anything from someone who incessantly weaves my name into the sales pitch. This is a dusty and dated technique that originally was designed to build rapport. It's so overused, however, that it now comes off as insincere, and this is even true when it's done by seasoned communicators who usually get things pitch perfect. For instance, Cardinal Timothy Dolan, the archbishop of New York, is a skilled communicator, perhaps even gifted. He's to Boston's Cardinal Seán O'Malley what JFK was to Nixon, but when he did an on-air radio news interview about the recently inducted Pope Francis, he sounded more like a fabric salesman than a man of the cloth. He continually wove the reporter's name into his answers. If he'd done it once or twice, it wouldn't have been so noticeable. But he did it at least a dozen times in just five minutes. His answers sounded like this: "Well, Rich, . . ." "It's interesting you bring that up, Rich, . . ." "As you well know, Rich, . . ." Sounds like the archdiocese needs to update its media-training manual.

Say someone's name once, but don't insert anyone's name into the conversation more than that. They'll see through it.

I hope that all gives you a sense of relief, because I'm guessing that you've tried some of the bad communication advice I've just mentioned and it didn't work. Maybe you came away from the experience wondering what was wrong with you, mentally berating yourself for not being able to master the communication rule.

Let me tell you: you are not the problem. The advice you tried to follow is the problem.

You're about to learn a completely counterintuitive approach to communication. It will probably go against some of your instincts, and it will definitely be different from what you might have heard or read elsewhere.

For now, I'm going to ask you to trust me. Just read with an open mind. Consider each piece of advice. Practice it in low-key situations—at home, on friends, and on coworkers who won't gossip about you behind your back. I think you'll come to see, just as my clients have, that Pitch-Perfect communication is not just vital, it's also something anyone can learn.

2

THE PRINCIPLES OF PERSUASION

*When you do the common things in life in an uncommon
way, you will command the attention of the world.*
—GEORGE WASHINGTON CARVER

HOLDING YOUR AUDIENCE'S attention is like winning a tennis
match at Wimbledon. You better have a clearly defined strategy, execute it brilliantly, and muzzle any inner voice of self-doubt,
or you'll get crushed. And thanks to a number of complicating factors brought on by the times in which we live, winning is getting
harder.

For starters, we have a tortoise-and-hare-style speed disparity
that exists between our brains and our mouths. Your listener is capable of absorbing 400 words per minute, yet you are capable of
voicing only 125. So what does the human brain do when it is not
challenged to its full information-processing potential? It wanders
far off the trail you're verbally trying to blaze, which is why your
audience is hardwired to contemplate in the middle of your presentation such weighty issues as *Do I have enough milk for the morning?
Did I leave the iron on? I wonder if my daughter finished her science project. Is this guy kidding with his shirt-and-tie combination?*

And that's assuming that all 125 words we utter are efficient and
worthwhile. Factor in meaningless qualifiers or redundancy, and
you've got a recipe for listener boredom and disengagement. Per-

haps not surprisingly, only about 20 percent of what we say makes a lasting impact.

And the quest for listener engagement is only getting tougher. Research commissioned by Lloyds TSB Insurance shows that ten years ago, the average person could easily pay close attention for roughly twelve minutes. Now five minutes is more realistic. Why? Pinging, poking, tweeting, and Snapchatting have recalibrated our definition of sustained focus. Staccato snippets of constant communication in the form of texts, tweets, e-mails, and ten-second voice memos bombard us, with the average person being exposed to five thousand messages a day. As a result, our collective attention spans seem to be shrinking faster than the ozone layer. Distraction and mental multitasking are now a way of life.

Here's another trend working against us: researchers from the University of Grenada have determined that healthier, fitter people tend to more easily pay attention than unhealthy, out-of-shape people. Not surprising. I can't say I've ever felt mentally sharp right after Thanksgiving dinner. All that energy needed to break down and digest your food must be diverted from your brain. So if there is a correlation between our expanding waistlines and our shrinking attention spans, the lecture circuit in America could be doomed.

As attention deficits grow, the techniques we use to keep people's attention need to be more and more effective. Learning how to be Pitch Perfect has never been more important.

THE ATROPHY OF VERBAL COMMUNICATION

Millions of years from now, when archaeologists find our fossils, they will no doubt be able to deduce that our thumbs grew large and powerful as a result of our constant use of mobile devices (ironic, because what we really need are *smaller* thumbs). Perhaps they will also discover a scoliosis-type condition in our upper spines from being constantly hunched over those digital screens.

I'm guessing they will also observe vocal cords that are almost completely atrophied, for the art of spoken communication seems endangered. At the risk of taking liberties with the well-used slogan that tripped up Dan Quayle in 1988, the art of spoken communication is a terrible thing to waste, and like any unused muscle, it will grow weak and flabby.

Once upon a time, the menu of communication methods for the average person was pretty short: speaking and letter writing. Recently, I marveled over the fact that a Gen Y friend of mine received an actual letter in the mail, with a stamp and everything. I was momentarily reassured by this retro gesture, until I found out that the sender was in a rehab facility where digital devices were not allowed.

Today, as my friends in Silicon Valley would say, technology has completely disrupted traditional communication. The wealth of alternative communication options has drastically curtailed the amount of time we devote each day to actually speaking.

It's not unlike a scenario from the childhood of us Baby Boomers. Those of you my age or older probably remember your parents standing in front of you, hands on hips, as you sat there slack-jawed in front of the boob tube in your fourth straight hour of mindless absorption. They shouted, "Your brain's going to rot if you keep watching that thing. Pick up a book and read something!"

I'm sure we share the same lament: If only I knew back then how right they were. You can read J. D. Salinger's *Catcher in the Rye* twenty-five times and come away with something new every time. It would be hard to make the same claim about multiple viewings of an episode of *Laverne and Shirley*. After years of exposure to mass media wastelands like *My Favorite Martian* and *The Brady Bunch*, it's a miracle that I can even write this book.

What TV was to books, digital devices are to the spoken word.

End result: An already weak communications muscle gets even weaker. And like smoking cigarettes or dining at McDonald's daily, we know this behavior isn't good for us, but somehow we just can't help ourselves.

If you're a Millennial, part of the generation that is unquestionably the most tech savvy, there's ample motivation for kicking the habit and practicing how people communicated "back in the day." Taking a more traditional approach just might determine your professional success. According to research commissioned by the global accounting firm Ernst & Young, the numbers of Millennials taking on management roles in 2013 grew 87 percent, as compared with 38 percent for Gen X and 19 percent for Baby Boomers. But when asked who is equipped to manage most effectively in today's climate, Millennials lagged way behind their older counterparts in perceived competency: only 27 percent, as opposed to 76 percent of Baby Boomers and 80 percent of Gen Xers. The E&Y research showed that "Gen Y is currently the least skilled at displaying executive presence." Effective communication is a major component of this characteristic. The research pointed to "clear, concise and frequent conversations" as being the key to getting past misunderstandings and preconceived notions.

You might be tempted to argue, What's the big deal? If I'm still as effective and much more comfortable when I communicate through writing, why do I need to learn how to do it while talking?

Here's why: Quality literature notwithstanding, spoken communication conveys so much more than writing because of our ability to clarify our words with intonation. If you've ever had one of your text messages misunderstood by a friend, you know that, when tone is lost, it's difficult to decipher the true meaning of written communication. But it's not just nuance that gets sacrificed. In our give-it-to-me-in-a-one-pager culture, there's always the chance that your written message was never absorbed in the first place. How many times has someone asked you a question that you've already answered several times by e-mail? How often has one of your supervisors asked you to add something to a report that is already in the report? How many times have you hit the DELETE button on e-mails, texts, and other forms of written communication after giving them only a cursory skim or no skim at all?

More times than you can put a number on, right?

NO ONE GRADUATES FROM ELOQUENCE SCHOOL

I found that my clients didn't always believe me when I insisted that even accomplished public speakers must continue to prepare just as diligently and rehearse just as thoroughly as they did when they were less experienced. The first presidential debate of 2012 changed all that.

President Obama's debate team set up shop in Las Vegas and was primed for some rigorous prep sessions. There was just one problem. Their star pupil wasn't terribly engaged. He cut short one practice session for a trip to Hoover Dam and passed on watching video of Mitt Romney's performance in debates against his Republican rivals. After a couple of days of this troubling trend, David Axelrod, the president's chief campaign advisor, spoke up. He told Obama that he was concerned that he didn't seem focused and that his rehearsals lacked intensity. The president's response was "Don't worry, I'm a game-time player. I'll be there at game time." Well, we all know that the self-proclaimed game-time player shot nothing but air balls during that first debate. By all accounts—liberal and conservative—Obama didn't just lose the first debate against Romney, he got shellacked. His poor performance made his lead in the polls evaporate overnight, and as a result, he spent the rest of the campaign trying to undo the damage.

The debacle was a startling reminder that even elite communicators can't mail it in. There's no magic switch you flip in your back to suddenly turn on oratorical greatness. No matter who you are, you have to put in the time. Even the Secretary of 'Splainin' Things, Bill Clinton, continues to work at it. One of the key members of his communications team once told me that adequate prep was essential for the former president. "Hands down, the best communicator I've ever seen . . . when he was prepared. But when his schedule got superchaotic and his available prep time was compromised, it always showed."

In addition to a lack of time to prepare and rehearse, one of the other perils of great communicators is overconfidence. Many people mistakenly think that just because they regularly speak in public, they will be there at game time, as Obama so misguidedly thought.

This is a bad habit to get into, especially if you're a senior executive. Once you've attained that level within a company, most of your subordinates are powerless to tell you the truth—perhaps that your remarks lack focus or that your delivery feels dry. In all my years coaching public speakers, I've never heard someone descend from a podium after a mediocre speech and get a truthful answer to the question, "How did I do?"

That's where I come in. Think of me as the antidote to the corporate sycophants who suck up to the C-suite execs by telling them how great they are. My job is to tell clients what they need to hear without mortally wounding their egos. I try to dole out honesty in a reaffirming and constructive way that allows them to retain their dignity. But every once in a while a different tack is required. For instance, bright and early one Monday morning, a corporate executive walked into the room I had set up for media training. The door had barely shut behind her when she began complaining: "What's all this about? Who set this up? I don't need media training! I'm good in dealing with reporters! I don't have time for this! I have a project due at noon today . . . whose idea was this?"

Hers was a full-fledged, neck-vein-popping tirade, and all before she ever allowed me to utter a sound. Eventually she needed to take a breath, so she demanded an explanation. "I mean what can you possibly teach me that I don't already know?"

Now my normal instinct is to appease. But in this instance, I made a split-second decision that the Pitch-Perfect response was akin to throwing a glass of cold water in her face. I answered her question, and in as calm a voice as I could muster, I said, "Well, the vibe you give off to reporters is extremely important to get them to strike a tone in their piece that's favorable to you. If you irk them, the piece can turn out snarky. If you're warm and embracing of the process, they'll likely give you the benefit of the doubt. And establishing that good chemistry has everything to do with savvy interpersonal social skills, the type you're *not* demonstrating right now."

Her mouth opened, but no words came out. For a second, it was the adult equivalent of a small child's moment of hesitation between taking a nasty fall and screaming. I quickly looked over at her handler, who had joined us, from the company's corporate communications department. His cheeks had lost all their color. Rather than wait for her to respond, I calmly kept going with specific techniques for how to establish that rapport. Four hours later, the executive was insisting to her PR handler that everyone in her department go through this same training. There's no outcome sweeter than that.

I've rarely met someone whose communication muscle couldn't be a bit more toned. I've also never met someone who is hopeless. So no matter where you are in the communications continuum, take heart in knowing that you can get better.

THE GREAT COMMUNICATION GAP

The aspect of my business I love the most is the sheer diversity of clients. We've had everyone from former gang members who were violent felons on the toughest streets in America to the greatest living jazz musician to Super Bowl MVPs.

And the takeaway? Everyone communicates differently. Thank goodness. Imagine how boring it would be otherwise. Some people come to us with many strengths. They might need just a quick tune-up. Others are not as practiced, and they need a lot more training. Many are strong in some communication areas but weak in others.

In the dozen or so years I've been training clients, women have constituted about 65 percent of our clientele. There are a number of reasons for this. Most of the women leaders I've met and worked with are devoted to self-improvement. They rarely let their egos get in the way of acknowledging that someone else might have some valuable guidance to impart. As a result, they are an absolute joy to coach.

But an obvious communication gender gap persists in the business world, and it's a disparity our company devotes a fair amount of time to closing. A woman communicating in the workplace is not unlike a gymnast navigating a balance beam. Many do it with skill, precision, and grace. But damn, that sucker seems awfully narrow sometimes, leaving little room for error. How easy it is to lose your balance on one side by being too conciliatory, empathetic, and equivocating. Swing back too far on the other side, and you'll be accused of being humorless, cold, bossy, and inflexible—the very qualities that, when displayed by men, are seen as strong leadership attributes. Too big a swing in either direction means you've probably fallen off the beam and are picking yourself up off the mat.

Many of the women I've worked with get this balance just right. They are able to be assertive and unapologetic in their verbal communication while maintaining an optimistic, warm, and inspiring demeanor. The same tough, opinionated, no-nonsense message delivered with a schoolmarmish scowl doesn't earn anyone a perfect 10. Chances are, your scores will be higher if your message is delivered with a brighter expressiveness.

But some women leaders struggle, often because they are sensitive to how they think others perceive them. Being aware of the vibe in the room is a good thing, in moderation, but you can't let it consume you to the point of distraction. I find I must often remind the women I coach, "Don't care so much what people think!"

Here's why. Playing the role of pleaser sets you too far back on your heels and distracts you from the task at hand. Plus, most of us are terrible mind readers. Some people seem completely bored, confused, or annoyed even when they are actually anything but. Once, during a presentation of mine, I couldn't help but notice a man in the back row whose thumbs were in overdrive on his BlackBerry. During a short break, I said to him, "I hope you're not dealing with some emergency back at the office." To my delight, he said, "Oh no, I'm just really good at taking notes on my Black-Berry." So now when I see the tops of people's heads in the audience and the light from their screens reflecting off their faces, I convince myself that they're taking copious notes. Why should you allow any other thought to compromise your confidence?

In general, I've found that the women I work with are more susceptible to internalizing these apparent slights, which affects their performance. It seems harder for them to silence that evil little voice that whispers, *You're bombing up here.* That voice convinces many women that everyone in the audience is waiting for a screwup so they can start tweeting about the horribly boring talk they are being forced to sit through.

I tell women that, in truth, more often than not, the audience is silently rooting for them to do well. I remind them that Winston Churchill said, "You'll never get to your destination if you stop to throw stones at every dog that barks."

Don't misunderstand me. Men suffer from speaking nerves, too. But they seem to be able to more easily focus on their message rather than how they are being perceived. As a result, most men will generally come right out and tell you what they think and then support that view with a story, statistics, or proof. That's definitely a plus. Women, in an effort to limit the likelihood that their point of view will be discredited or criticized, tend to give the airtight support for their idea before revealing the actual idea. In short, they tend to back into their message with less conviction.

While men might be more direct, they have their own challenges. They tend not to be as empathetic as women and, as a result, are not naturally as skilled at explaining how something helps their customers, clients, or listeners. In business, we offer services and create products that solve problems in people's lives. Compared with women, men are not as good at articulating the frustrations and limitations of how life was before a service or product was created.

FOUR TYPES OF POOR COMMUNICATORS

In addition to the differences between men and women, I also have found that people communicate differently in several other ways. Below are just four examples.

The BACKSPACE Button Pressers

I coach many writers, journalists, and authors, and it fascinates me just how many of them speak the way they write. Writers typically construct a sentence, evaluate it, and, if they think they can improve on it, they will peck away at the BACKSPACE key and tweak it. That works great when you are sitting in front of a keyboard, but many people do it while they are talking, too. A few lines from a BACKSPACE Button Presser's mouth might sound like this: "I was in California. I think it was northern California. And I was driving . . . well, actually, I was the passenger. My friend was driving. Anyway, we were going to this conference. Well, it was more like a meeting. . . ."

When speaking, go easy on the BACKSPACE button. It can create a frustratingly halting way of communicating in which the stutter step is more prevalent than the smooth glide forward. The first way things come out of your mouth is usually the best. Resist the urge to self-edit to make the less-vital information 100 percent precise.

The Minutiae Lovers

Many people tend to get caught up in the minutiae of what they've built rather than explaining what the consumer can do with this wonderful invention. Consumers don't want to know about the process of how something came into existence. What they want to know is: How will this product change my life? How will it help me?

The Expounders

Rather than making a point quickly and then moving on, an Expounder mentions the same point over and over again. I see this most often when coaching instructors and professors. College courses are challenging. Professors stand at the front of a lecture hall and fill fifty-plus minutes (and compete with Millennials hooked on their digital devices). That's not a great environment in which to practice brevity. This setting can sometimes be all about filling time. Professors expound and embellish and drive points home over and over again. That may work in academia, but it's not ideal in the real world.

The Cliché Champs

Most people abuse clichés at some point, but athletes, for some reason, rely on them almost exclusively. Somewhere they're taught that the answer to every question should be thirty to forty seconds long, should be filled with clichés, and should communicate absolutely nothing. In the film *Bull Durham*, Kevin Costner's character, Crash Davis, counsels a teammate who is on the verge of being promoted to the major leagues and thus subject to media interviews. "You're gonna have to learn your clichés. You're gonna have to study them, you're gonna have to know them. They're your friends. Write this down: 'We gotta play it one day at a time.'" Every once in a while, a player comes along who gives interesting, original quotes. Curtis Granderson of the New York Yankees is one example. When asked recently about the spate of injuries and reinjuries plaguing his team, Granderson said, "I think we've got to find whoever's got this voodoo doll and just keeps poking at it, ripping at it."

THE SEVEN PRINCIPLES

No matter how toned or flabby your verbal communication muscle, the Seven Principles of Persuasion can help you get into game shape.

Originally the principles were merely a mental checklist that I kept during the several years when I worked as a television news correspondent and later as a producer. In those jobs, I interviewed thousands and thousands of people and, as a result, edited countless hours of audio and video. Any one interview might result in thirty to forty minutes of tape, which I had to trim down to a one-minute portion that kept viewers' attention. In the editing room, I learned to let the sound just travel past my ears—ignoring everything that seemed long-winded, inconsequential, boring, mundane, excessive, and ordinary. When I heard something that was engaging, interesting, and provocative, however, my ears suddenly came alive, because I knew I had my sound bite.

Over time, as I edited enough tape, I realized that the best sound bites and segments all followed seven important principles.

The Headline Principle

Get attention by starting with your best material, especially a grabbing, thought-provoking line that makes listeners think, *I want to know more.* Don't bury the lead. Don't copy others. Don't resort to clichéd formulas. Don't ease into a point. Start with a concise and compelling statement.

The Scorsese Principle

Hold attention with visual images that illustrate a story. I think most who have seen Martin Scorsese's film *Goodfellas* remember the scene of Paul Sorvino thinly slicing a garlic clove with a razor blade in prison. That visual illustrated the gourmet lifestyle his wiseguys were living even behind bars. Through your words, craft stories that are so engaging that the listener is hanging on every detail. Direct the film that plays in your listener's mind.

The Pasta-Sauce Principle

Cure boredom by boiling down your message, making it as rich and brief as possible. When in doubt, cut more out. If people want more, they'll ask for seconds.

The No-Tailgating Principle

The speed with which you talk should be directly proportional to how certain you are about the next sentence coming out of your mouth. The more certain you are, the more briskly you can choose to speak. But if you're prone to saying the first thing that pops into your head, a slower pace with strategic pausing is a sure way to prevent your mouth from tailgating your brain. And as with automobiles, when the lead car stops short from uncertainty of where to go next, it's likely that the tailgater trailing behind will crash into the one in front. The verbal equivalent of a crash is filler: like, um, you know, etc. And et cetera, for that matter.

The Conviction Principle

Convey certainty with words, eye contact, posture, and tone of voice.

The Curiosity Principle

The best broadcast interviewers earn trust by displaying genuine interest, as if there is nowhere else they'd rather be. They demonstrate this by maintaining an engaged facial expression. One of the reasons viewers loved the former *Meet the Press* anchor Tim Russert was because you could see on his face how much he really loved his job. He exuded an "I can't believe I get paid to do this" demeanor. He could ask tough questions but seemed warm rather than obnoxious as he did so. As a result, his questions never seemed low-blow- or gotcha-style.

The Draper Principle

Don Draper, in case you don't know, is the fictional character from the hit AMC show *Mad Men*. He plays the creative director of a Manhattan advertising firm and is known for his effectiveness at pitching ideas. I based the final principle on him because I believe it's one he would teach you himself if he were not in fact a work of fiction. The best way to stay on point is to make sure the flow and focus of the discussion plays to your strengths. If it strays elsewhere, away from an area in which you can shine, transition it back. It's the ole Don Draper adage, "If you don't like what's being said, change the conversation."

When I left television journalism and began training clients for media interviews, I taught them the seven principles. At first the networks bristled at the notion that their interview subjects would be coached. They thought that kind of preparation would make interviewees seem stilted and rehearsed. Now they view it differently. They realize that with the right kind of media training, the talking heads or characters in their segments will deliver sound bites and visual storytelling that is memorable. The principles have worked so well that it's not unusual for the networks to call and ask how the training is going with the character they are planning to interview the following week.

Over time, I realized that the principles worked not just for media interviews; they worked for nearly every communication situation. I taught them to clients who wanted to hone their public-speaking skills, shine as a moderator or guest on a panel, or score a perfect 10 on their next job interview.

Pretty soon the principles were making their way into every coaching session. But they're also immensely helpful away from the office, when family and friends ask for advice on what to say in certain social and professional situations.

Frequently my clients stay in touch and tell me about their successes. What's interesting is that nearly all of them have said that the principles I've taught them for one initial purpose—whether it was to deliver a speech or to shine on the *Today* show—apply to nearly everything they do at work. They use these principles when communicating with anyone about anything.

As one CEO recently told me, "You know that technique you taught me about maintaining a curious and engaged facial expression on camera? I use it now whenever my employees are giving me a report in an internal meeting. Now that I look interested and welcoming, they deliver it more concisely and more confidently. I used to look at them with a furrowed brow because I was concentrating, but this caused them to lose confidence, feel the need to overexplain everything, speak in circles, and waste time."

Similarly, I taught an executive of a major PR firm an important technique for moderating panel discussions. She was then able to use it to bring in new business. Panel moderators must be able to subtly and discreetly keep "panel hogs" from sucking up all the available oxygen in the room. The last thing a moderator wants to do is awkwardly wrestle control back from them in a way that screams "I cut him off." This executive found herself in a similar situation during a new business pitch. One of her junior employees, mistakenly thinking she was on a roll, was going on way too long, engaging in acute TMI and talking herself and the firm out of an account. Rather than do nothing and allow the damage to be done, the executive deftly took the baton from her chatty subordinate and wrapped things up while the pitch still had a chance of ending up in the win column.

One job candidate recently wrote to us saying that the same technique we taught him to prepare for a job interview (one that helped him nail a top-level job at Google) also helped him prepare for a five-minute speech at a friend's wedding, one that happened to be held in Japan. He delivered his speech in Japanese, a language he'd never before studied. "It turned out being one of the top five experiences of my life," he said.

This continual feedback made me realize that the presentation skills I teach clients are universal and apply to all important personal and professional situations. When used, the Seven Principles of Persuasion send a message that you are open, interested, receptive, confident, and smart. You are better able to convince people around you to listen to, take note of, and act on what you say.

Despite their importance and universality, few people know about these principles, and even fewer understand how to use them. That's because many of the principles are counterintuitive. For instance, the less you say, the more people hear and remember. That's the Pasta-Sauce Principle. Yet all too often, people do the opposite, relying on the outdated and ineffective management-consulting way of communicating: Tell 'em what you're going to tell 'em. Tell 'em. And then tell 'em what you told 'em. They go on and on, making the same point, hoping that, by the third time they've said the same sentence, everyone in the room will believe it. In reality, there's no better way to demonstrate that your approach is outdated.

Similarly, many people know that they ought to omit filler words—the *ums* and *ahs* between their sentences. Yet they can't seem to stop using these words. They also know that eye contact is important, yet they continually find themselves staring at the floor or closing their eyes as they talk. And they've been told to sound confident, but few know that the secret behind accomplishing that lies in how you formulate your thoughts and speech patterns.

Throughout the pages of *Pitch Perfect*, you'll learn how to overcome all of these bad communication habits. The beauty of the Principles of Persuasion is that they are as easy to learn, implement, and master as they are effective. Simply by slowing down your speech, for instance, you'll more easily omit those filler words I mentioned earlier. Similarly, as part of the Conviction Principle, we teach you not just the power postures to use while standing or sitting, but also the optimal structure in which to convey your thoughts. In this way, you will both look confident and feel confident.

HOW TO LEARN THE PRINCIPLES

Most of my clients are able to grasp most of the Seven Principles of Persuasion in just half a day and soon after put them into practice in different areas of their lives. It's my hope that you'll master them as quickly too.

For best results:

- Focus on one principle and one aspect of a principle at a time. Don't overwhelm yourself by trying to perfectly apply every piece of advice at once.

- As you learn about each principle, study those around you. Watch television news segments with a more critical eye, and pay close attention to *how* speakers hold and lose your attention. See if you can pinpoint where and when various speakers use a principle to hold attention. Dissect their performance and think about what you want to emulate and avoid.
- Study yourself. I record video of my clients during sessions and play it back for them. Sure, some people cringe when they see themselves onscreen, but I've found that this is one of the most efficient ways for people to improve. So record your phone calls. Watch yourself as you conduct Skype sessions. Ask a trusted friend to record you during presentations. Use the video-recording feature on your smartphone or tablet when you're rehearsing your presentation. The more playback you review, the easier it will be for you to see where you are using the principles well and where you could stand to improve.
- Study this book. To help you learn these principles quickly, I've modeled them in the writing of *Pitch Perfect*. Every chapter uses the Headline Principle—just as I have done with the overview of this suggestion. Along the way, I've employed the Scorsese Principle, continually using visual storytelling to illustrate and support each point. See if you can spot the principles on the pages.

I promise you that soon, rather than fear high-stakes situations, you'll look forward to them. Rather than find them terrifying, you'll feel a sense of exhilaration. When you use the Principles of Persuasion to your advantage, you'll feel confident and at peace as you win the client, nail the job interview, or deliver the best speech of your life.

3

THE HEADLINE PRINCIPLE

On average, five times as many people read the headline as read the body copy. When you have written your headline, you have spent eighty cents out of your dollar.

—DAVID OGILVY

THERE ARE SIX words that have an unparalleled capacity to raise your blood pressure regardless of where you work: "The boss wants to see you." They generate much the same internal response as when your older siblings used to say, "Mom and Dad are going to *kill* you." So when those words came down from the executive producer's office at *A Current Affair*, not even deep yogic breathing could slow my runaway pulse. With my arm casually resting against the doorframe of his office, I asked, "You wanted to see me?" I tried to say it casually, but I think my voice cracked.

He was standing behind his desk, hunched over the Nielsen ratings printout, which was undoubtedly putting him in a foul mood. He raised his head and with a forced smile said, "Shut the door." I had seen that facial expression before. It's not unlike the one Goldfinger flashed right before his laser weapon almost castrated James Bond.

I reminded myself to stay calm. I was now standing across from a guy whose popularity rating was, to quote my old buddy Matt Lauer, "lower than polio." My stress was compounded by the obvious: my contract with the show was up for renewal. For people like Maury Povich, the show's anchor and a recognized name in TV, an expiring contract was like Christmas: "Yes, I'd like a 50 percent salary increase, incentive clauses, stock options, a personal driver, first-class travel on out-of-town stories. That's good for starters. Now let's talk about the designer wardrobe I'll be getting."

I wasn't a Maury, not by a long shot. Yes, I was one of the show's original members, and my segments often had a certain signature style and tone, but in TV land, that and $2.50 could get you on the subway. I never deluded myself that the average person in Nebraska could pick me out of a tabloid-TV lineup. As my extremely wise and talented agent, Wayne Kabak, had told me over lunch, "If you're not a household name by the age of forty, you're always going to be playing a game of diminishing returns. There's always the chance that they'll find someone younger and cheaper to do what you do, calculating that the drop-off in quality apparent to the audience will be minimal."

Suddenly, at thirty-one, forty wasn't something I needed binoculars to see. Were my returns going to start diminishing in this meeting? I loved this gig and was not ready to see it end. The walk from the doorway to his desk was only a few feet, but it felt much longer. Now, looking back down at the ratings sheet, he motioned dismissively to the chairs on the other side of his desk, saying, "Sit down." His tone made it sound more like, "You better sit down for this."

My boss took a deep breath and then said, "So as you know, your contract is about to come to an end, and we've been thinking very carefully of who on this show has been pulling their weight and making a valuable contribution. We've analyzed which reporters have led the way in terms of quantity and quality of stories, and we've measured how you compare against your colleagues. As you know, this is a very competitive field with dozens of audition tapes coming into our offices every day from people who are dying to do what you do."

I could barely pay attention to what he was saying because I was already wondering whether it was too late to cancel that summer vacation for the family I had just booked.

My boss went on like that for another fifteen to thirty seconds. Then he finally said, "So weighing all those factors, we've decided to offer you a new contract that will keep you here another three years."

My first reaction was, of course, relief, followed shortly thereafter by an insatiable urge to choke the life from this guy. Why had he kept me dangling on the edge that long? My colleagues and I suspected that he derived some sick pleasure from watching others twist in the wind.

Most people, though, don't delay making their point with such malevolent intent. They do it completely by accident. However, postponing your reveal and getting off to a slow start rarely works in your favor. That's why the expression "It's not how you start, it's how you finish that matters" does not apply to public speaking and conversations. Fumble your start during any Pitch-Perfect situation, and you render the finish irrelevant. Nobody will be around to hear you.

The first thirty seconds of any conversation or presentation are like the last two minutes of a football game. This is when victory or defeat is determined, the period of time when your audience is deciding whether you are interesting enough for them to continue paying attention. Say just the right thing, and the communication game is yours. Your audience gets hooked, and they're enticed to hear what you will say next. Get it wrong, and your listeners start daydreaming, checking their smartphones, or plotting their conversational exit strategy.

Unfortunately, more speakers get it wrong than right.

HOW NOT TO OPEN A CONVERSATION

Through osmosis we've all learned a bland predictable way of starting conversations and presentations, which has unfortunately become the template for public speaking.

Consider the following clichéd ways speakers open their presentations.

Agenda Setting

The most common mistake I hear throughout all corporate America is the ubiquitous and übertedious agenda-setting start (calling it by its acronym would actually be quite fitting). Here's how an ASS sounds:

"Good morning. I'd like to spend some time this morning talking about the key strategies behind overcoming the anxieties that accompany public speaking. We'll look at some examples of people who are proficient at this and people who are challenged from a performance perspective. And then we'll take a deeper dive into what makes for effective communication from a strategic standpoint. But before we do that, I'd like to just take a step back and just very quickly walk you through some considerations that are good to keep in mind prior to any external communications opportunity."

Sound familiar? I'm sure it does. The overwhelming majority of presentations start this way, and it's one of the hardest habits to get clients to break.

Yet the ASS is clunky and dull. There's no quicker way to get your audience wondering whether they remembered to close their garage door or daydreaming about the Twix bar they're going to break into after this awful meeting is over.

You might think, "Everyone else does it." That's true. There are even respected consulting firms that have long been proponents of this public-speaking strategy:

Tell 'em what you're going to tell 'em.

Tell 'em.

Tell 'em what you told 'em.

With all due respect to the consulting big boys, I'm not a fan of this strategy. In fact, I think it's dusty, outdated, and predictable. That's precisely why you don't want to use the ASS. If you start off sounding like everyone else, your audience immediately assumes there's nothing fresh and original in your presentation—same ol', same ol'. Because you're packaging it in a form the audience has heard a gazillion times, your listeners think, *Been here, heard that.*

Clock Watching

Similar to agenda setting, clock watching lets the listener know just how long you'll be talking. This is a mistake for all the reasons I mentioned under agenda setting and more. Chances are, you are not giving your listeners information they don't already know. So why waste time telling them? Worse, mentioning the length of your talk only reinforces the idea that your listeners will be digitally cut off from the rest of the world, a thought that makes us twitch like people in detox.

In preparation for a training session recently, I was screening video footage of the person I was to coach as he delivered his last presentation. His first sentence began, "For the next three hours . . ." Wow! Talk about an interest-killer. The last thing any audience wants to be reminded of is that it will be captive for longer than your average Oliver Stone movie.

Gratuitous Gratitude

Gratitude has a place, but don't spend the first full minute of your remarks thanking a long laundry list of people. If you must convey thanks—for instance to your superiors—do it quickly and then view what comes after your thanks as your true headliner.

The Buried Lead

Nearly all presentations could be drastically improved with one quick and simple edit: lopping off the first two paragraphs. Try it. You'll be amazed at how engaging an abrupt start can be. Why slowly build to making your point when providing an unexpected jolt to your audience works so much better?

"I'm So Excited, and I Just Can't Hide It!"

Excited has become the most overused word in the speaking world, and most people say "I'm so excited to be here" in a tone of voice that conveys anything but. It has become the most gratuitous, obligatory thing to say, and it has long ceased having any effect, especially when it's said without the slightest hint of a smile. I am not exaggerating when I tell you that sometimes I hear it three times in just the first sentence: "I'm so excited to be here at what is such an exciting time for our company, and I know you're all excited about what the future holds."

Falling Flat with Stand-Up

It doesn't matter whether it's Ricky Gervais or Jon Stewart—none of those guys ever tries out new material live on stage, and you shouldn't either. Jokes are incredibly hard to pull off, as Don West, a defense attorney for George Zimmerman, learned in 2013. Zimmerman was accused of second-degree murder for the fatal shooting of Trayvon Martin. During his opening remarks, West said, "I think the evidence will show that this is a sad case. . . . Sometimes you have to laugh to keep from crying. So let me, at considerable risk . . . I'd like to tell you a little joke. I know that may sound a little weird in this context and under these circumstances, but I think you are the perfect audience for it. . . . Here it goes. Knock knock. Who's there? George Zimmerman. George Zimmerman who? All right, good. You're on the jury." When no one laughed, West responded, "Nothing? That's funny. . . ." He did go on to win the trial, but he'll forever be known as the lawyer who told the bad knock-knock joke.

Unless it has gotten laughs every single one of the twenty times you've told it, leave jokes to professional comedians, especially if they have nothing to do with your presentation. You would be much better off telling a funny story that directly relates to your remarks. A brilliant example of this occurred during a TED Talk in 2013 on education by Geoffrey Canada, the cofounder of the Harlem Children's Zone. His opening thirty seconds had the audience laughing, loosened up, and hungry to hear more:

> I'm a little nervous because my wife, Yvonne, said to me, "Geoff, you watch the TED Talks," and I said, yes, honey, I love TED Talks. She said, "You know they're like really smart, talented. . . ." [audience laughs] I said I know, I know. She said, "You know, they don't want . . . the angry black man." [audience erupts in laughter] So I said, no, I'm going to be good, honey, I'm going to be good. [pause] But I am angry. And the last time I looked . . . [he looks down at the color of the skin on the back of his hand]

Here's what makes this open so incredibly effective:

1. He is not telling a joke, but rather a funny story.
2. The audience members feel that they have access to Geoffrey, because he has admitted vulnerability (the fact that he's ner-

vous) and he has let them eavesdrop on a personal conversation between him and his wife.

3. His punch line, that he is angry, is not just the payoff to the story. Instead, it represents the main theme of the talk that follows, that he is angry that education reform has made little progress over the past fifty years.

Your Conformity Zone

As a general rule, if everyone else is doing it, you *don't* want to do it. Starting off a presentation or conversation the way everyone else starts them makes your listeners think, *I've heard this a million times*. Although your content will be different, the packaging upfront is the same, causing your listeners to sink into their chairs.

BEING PITCH PERFECT MEANS NEVER HAVING TO SAY YOU'RE SORRY

The ninth-worst way to open a presentation is so pervasive that it deserves its own section: apology. I'm amazed at how many people apologize at the beginning of their presentations. Based on what I've witnessed over the years, there appears to be no good time to give a presentation, for at one time or another, I've heard all of the following:

Nine a.m.: The Sleepyhead Apology. "Good morning. I know it's early and everybody was out late partying last night, but stay with me here the best you can."

Eleven a.m.: The Growling-Stomach Apology. "So I know it's been a long morning and everyone's starting to get hungry for lunch, but I want to take just a little bit of your time."

One p.m.: The Just-Fed-and-Lazy Apology. "I know everyone just had a big lunch and you're probably all dreaming of taking a siesta, so I promise to try to keep this lively."

Three p.m.: The Blood-Sugar-Crash Apology. "Everybody feeling that midafternoon energy swoon? Well, I'm going to try to take your mind off that sugar fix you're probably craving."

Five p.m.: The "When's Cocktail Hour?" Apology. "It's been a long day, and I know I'm the only thing standing between you and Happy Hour, but I'm just going to quickly walk you through . . ."

Recently I gave a presentation to the media group of a major publishing company during perhaps the least desirable time slot: eleven thirty a.m. It also happened to be on the final day of a two-day conference—in other words, right before lunch and a just a few hours before everyone's flight home. The sight of packed luggage and the sound of grumbling stomachs were everywhere when I walked into the auditorium, not to mention bloodshot eyes from the company party the night before. In the world of public speaking, facing an audience with this toxic trifecta can be a real confidence killer.

So I decided to address it. "Imagine just for a moment that you are in my shoes, right here, right at this moment. How many of you would consider starting by acknowledging that you are the last speaker on the program, it's right before lunch, many are tired and possibly still hungover from last night's party, and all you really want to do is get a move on so you don't have to rush to catch your flight?"

About three quarters of my listeners raised their hands, thinking that would be the right strategy.

"You would be dead wrong," I said to the shocked and now suddenly attentive crowd. You never want to apologize to any audience, thus planting the notion that people are going to be counting the minutes until you're done. Even subtly hinting that they may have something else they'd rather be doing is Ambien for your audience.

PITCH-PERFECT MAKEOVER

I worked with an executive just before he would be attending a dinner with many female CEOs and delivering some introductory remarks.

WHAT HE PLANNED TO SAY
"Thank you so much for being here. I know some of you come from great distances during a time of year when travel can be a real chore."

WHAT I COACHED HIM TO SAY
"New York at Christmastime is magical. I don't know how many of you have noticed, but I really could have used some of that magic as I was trying to get across town through the traffic, which coincided with the lighting of the tree. Some of you traveled many miles to get here, and some of you felt as if you did just to get across town. To all of you: thank you."

TALK LIKE A JOURNALIST

I've given you plenty of ways *not* to start your presentation. What's a better approach? Well, think of how a journalist writes a news story. Good journalists put their most compelling material in the first paragraph, known as the lead. This is the sentence or paragraph that grabs the readers or viewers, enticing them to want more. An effective lead is often surprising—even counterintuitive. It makes the reader think, *What's this about? I want to know more.*

I learned the importance of attention-grabbing leads when I was a reporter for *A Current Affair*. On days when I filled in as the show's anchor, I also wrote all the scripts to be read during the studio portions. That included the "teases," short snippets of copy that come just before a commercial break. We wanted those teases to discourage viewers from surfing other channels or getting up and leaving the room, even if it was to take a bathroom break. The teases had to be so good that viewers felt compelled to wait until the show resumed—because they couldn't wait to find out what happened next.

As you might imagine, writing teases took skill and creativity. Each tease included only a headline and a short follow-up sentence—just ten seconds of material in all. It also had to be clever and compelling. It had to entice the viewer.

When I became a communications coach, I realized that the elements of a good tease were the same as a good opening for a conversation or presentation.

Good teases generally have three characteristics:

1. **Short.** Convey it quickly, in just a line or two.
2. **Suspenseful.** Include an element of intrigue. Beginning your remarks with a story or some declarative, provocative statement works nicely. It gets your audience mentally chewing on something right away, which is what you want to accomplish. Make your audience wonder, "What does she mean by that?"
3. **Surprising.** Make your tease the opposite of a cliché, something that makes your listeners think, *This is new. I've never heard this before.* Do the unexpected and employ a different style. You'll get your audience leaning forward to hear what you have to say rather than slumping in their chairs to tune you out.

Not every opener includes all three traits, of course, but great openers include many of them.

Steve Jobs once opened a speech back in 1984 with the line, "Hi, I'm Steve Jobs." It was short, and it was also surprising. You wouldn't expect Jobs to introduce himself, considering that everyone in the auditorium knew him and had come specifically to hear him speak. After laughter and applause faded, he hooked his audience by immediately launching into a story: "It is 1958. IBM passes up the chance to buy a young, fledgling company that has invented a new technology called xerography." Notice that he did not start by saying, "I want to spend a little time this morning walking you through some of the historical context of the early days of personal computers and illustrate how it relates to Apple's current mission from an innovation perspective."

I don't want you spend hours and hours trying to force your opener into a three-S box. Just use the three S's as a guide and a source of inspiration that helps you find your best material. Here's one I have used in my own presentations that has seemingly done the trick:

"With amazing consistency every year, we human beings agree that three things scare the living hell out of us more than anything else in life. Ranked in order of the terror they instill, the first is dying, and the third is flying. And wedged right smack in the middle of those two is something that can reduce normally confident and accomplished people into neurotic cowards: it's public speaking. After today, you'll have to find another thing to fret about, because I want to strip the fear and anxiety out of something that can easily be an asset for you instead of a liability."

Yes, there is a line in there spelling out the intention of my presentation, but it comes after I've grabbed their attention, I hope. There's also a buildup to the reveal that it's public speaking occupying the number two position. Creating a little suspense with your audience by holding back the punch line can be an effective tactic. Try to build some anticipation around the delivery of your main point rather than just giving it away.

Sometimes I'll start with an analogy that leads quickly into an anecdote: "Public speaking is a lot like golf. The minute you think you've got it figured out and mastered, something comes along to humble you. I've learned this the hard way and was reminded of it just recently when something truly embarrassing happened to me in the middle of a presentation. I got blindsided because I over-looked one of the items on my prespeech checklist."

There isn't anyone in the audience at this point who isn't dying to know how I got my comeuppance. The payoff to this story is, no matter how good you get, you can't take preparation shortcuts, and then that leads me into my section on the steps you should take to prepare.

Here's something else I learned from writing for TV: you must grab your listener's attention more than once. Television is such a harsh environment. Viewers literally have devices in their hands that allow them to tune you out if they are even slightly bored.

As a result, I learned to write TV scripts that relentlessly held attention. Those scripts included an attention-grabbing opener fol-lowed by another attention-grabbing line roughly every twenty to thirty seconds.

You probably have a bit more leeway than we do on televi-sion, but the idea of continually grabbing your audience still ap-plies. Your opening headline grabs attention right away. To keep that attention, evenly disperse throughout your presentation the elements you think will be most engaging. Perhaps you have four different video clips you plan to show. Think about placing them at the two-, five-, eight-, eleven-, and fourteen-minute marks of a sixteen-to-eighteen-minute presentation.

PITCH-PERFECT MAKEOVER

Coming up with ways not to bury the lead is something I tend to work on more often with my female clients. For years, women in positions of authority have been held to superharsh and hyper-critical standards. They are frequently reluctant to display the same gravitas and certainty as their male counterparts for fear that their assertiveness will be harshly judged. So they tend to take a more tepid and conformist approach to their lead, which ultimately makes them seem less certain and less sure of themselves. Here is a before and after from one of my successful executive clients.

WHAT SHE PLANNED TO SAY

"Good Afternoon. It's so nice to be here." (Under her breath in the training session, she couldn't help admitting, "That's lame-o"). "So today we're going to take you through the ultimate potential for our brand . . . we have a great opportunity to present to you, along with all of the resources and capabilities needed.

"In order to give you context, we're going to take a look at our historical performance and at the five markets we've chosen to demonstrate our overall potential. This is a fabulous chart, and I'm very proud to report the degree of acceleration our brand has had both on the top line and the bottom line. We've almost tripled net sales by fiscal '13 with a corresponding growth in NOP from 12.4 percent to that magical number of almost 22 percent."

WHAT I COACHED HER TO SAY:

"Good afternoon. Phillip, Stanley, Sharon . . . we've been waiting for this day a long time. Right now, we have a great opportunity to grow our brand to that magical threshold of one billion dollars. Let me show you how we get there.

"First, some context. We've grown from $157 million in 2004, tripling the business since then, and—music to your ears—NOP has hit that target we all had hoped for: 22 percent."

The text doesn't convey the visual difference in her delivery. With the content shorter, crisper, and less rambling, she used her hands more, smiled more, and conveyed an air of certainty. It's interesting that she also removed her glasses between take one and take two, which seemed to further perk up her delivery.

WHERE GREAT HEADLINES LURK

Clients often have plenty of great headline material, but they don't know it. During a training session, they sometimes start off with clichéd openers full of industryspeak and general monotony. Then, during a break, when they are feeling more relaxed, they say something like, "You'll never believe this. This one time . . ." Soon they are delivering a compelling story, one that holds my attention from their first word to the last.

When they finish, I wait a beat. Then I say, "That's your headline. That's what you should start with!"

Simply put, your headline is your best material. It's the lines that come after "You'll never believe this!" and "Oh, do I have a story for you!" and "Did you know that . . . ?"

When coming up with headlines, consider the stories you tell friends and coworkers as an aside, the ones that start, "You know, this funny thing happened" or "You will not believe what just happened."

Also look for strong statements, ones that you might be tempted to bury later in a conversation or speech. Many people make the mistake of building up to a provocative statement rather than leading with it. Often they'll be five minutes into their prepared material when I'll stop them and say, "The line that you just said? That's your opener."

They often reply, "Really? You want me to start there?"

Absolutely.

HOW TO TEST YOUR HEADLINE

Don't test out your headline during an important conversation or speech. Try it for the first time in a low-pressure situation. Test it out while gathered at the dinner table with people who are not your coworkers.

This is an especially great test if you have a teen or tween in the house. I know I'm being entertaining at the dinner table when I don't see heads looking down in the direction of their napkins (where we all know cell phones reside). If I can keep their faces up toward me, I know I've found my headline.

4

THE SCORSESE PRINCIPLE

The one thing you have that nobody else has is you. Your
voice, your mind, your story, your vision. So write and draw
and build and play and dance and live as only you can.

—Neil Gaiman

DISCOVERED THE SCORSESE Principle at age twenty-three, just after
I landed a big break and was hired as segment producer for a
prime-time infotainment TV show called *Two on the Town*. It was a
fluffy, feel-good show, during which nary a bad word was uttered
about anybody or anything. Think of it as the polar opposite of its
evil twin, *A Current Affair*, which I would call home a mere two
years later.

I'd gotten the job, I proudly assumed, based on the strength of
my writing test and the reel of stories I had helped produce during
my years at the local WCBS-TV News. On the contrary, as the executive producer later told me, "I needed to make some quick hires,
and I just figured you were a good Irish kid who wouldn't give me
any shit." Now you know how the recruitment wheels in TV turn.

When I say I had "helped" produce stories at WCBS, I mean just
that: I'd assisted. I was now a segment producer, but I'd never actually produced a segment on my own, and my bosses had no idea.

Day two on the new gig, my boss handed me a book and told
me to come back with a produced piece in two weeks. I looked

down at the cover: *The Art of Belly Dancing*. Was this some kind of gag? At first I thought they were putting me on. The minute I confirmed I hadn't been punk'd, I knew I was in trouble. Between knowing *zero* about the topic and having never actually produced a piece by myself, piloting a 747 solo would have been only slightly more intimidating. I was consumed with this sinking feeling that my maiden TV voyage might end up missing the runway and end in a catastrophic fireball.

Remember, this is 1984. There was no Internet and no magical website where I could type "how to produce a TV story" into the search field. And there was no way I was ever going to admit to my fellow producers that I needed help.

One week later, when my script was due, I found myself standing before Mike Rubin, the show's senior producer. A supersharp guy with a biting sense of humor, Mike's angular face and blank, penetrating listening expression seemed to communicate, "Are you some kind of idiot?"

"So let me see it," he said.

I handed Mike the script. Out came the red pencil, which to me looked like a lethal-injection syringe. It was then that I committed a rookie mistake: standing in the doorway of his office and watching him read it.

In less than a minute, his head slowly turned. He dropped his red pencil, leaned back, blankly looked up at the ceiling, exhaled, and said, "So I'm probably at the twenty- to thirty-second mark of your piece . . . , and instead of being glued to the TV, you know where I am right now, buddy? I'm in my kitchen making myself a peanut-butter sandwich."

I'd lost him. My piece was so punchless and tepid that he couldn't force himself to pay attention for longer than twenty seconds. Contemplating Skippy on Wonder Bread was ultimately much more appealing than reading the words of my dense, redundant, and pictureless script.

Mike eventually became a true mentor and a close friend. On that day, he taught me an important lesson, one that not only stuck with me throughout my career in television, but also pervades the advice I give to clients to this day: Visual storytelling is the sweet spot of good communication.

In this way, good communicators are a lot like film directors. They tell stories that paint visual pictures in the minds of their listeners. They provide rich detail but also manage to keep it tight.

According to a recent study, facts are twenty-two times more likely to be recalled when they are told in stories, and images are sixty thousand times more memorable than words. That's because humans are visual creatures. A movie reel is constantly spinning inside our brains. As a speaker, you want to be the director of that reel. If you illustrate your point with colorful stories your listeners can imagine, you will keep your listeners satiated—and satiated listeners are engaged listeners.

If, however, you veer off into abstraction and theory, the reel keeps playing, but now your listeners are creating their own films, which might have nothing to do with what you are saying. Rather than visualizing scenes directed by you, they are daydreaming about something completely unrelated.

PITCH-PERFECT POINTER

Want to be a great communicator? Try writing a screenplay. Even if your story is more hideous than the films *Ishtar* and *Gigli* combined, you'll learn how to capture and hold attention. That's because a screenplay forces you to make your point through visual description, action, or dialogue. Abstract or theoretical content is not allowed. The activity forces you to discover and develop visual storytelling.

THE ANTIDOTE TO BOREDOM

When I was young, two of my favorite shows were *The French Chef* with Julia Child and *The Galloping Gourmet* with Graham Kerr. Although Julia and Graham were stylistically quite different (Julia was easygoing and subtle, whereas Graham was wisecracking and bold), they shared one important characteristic: both chefs described their kitchen creations sensuously.

Words like *delicious* never entered the conversation. Consider how Julia described roast chicken: "From that marvelous aroma of roasting that fills the air to the first plunge of the knife down through its brown skin, the juices pearling at the break in the second joint as the carving begins, and finally that first mouthful, roast chicken has always been one of life's great pleasures."

Her words help you visualize every step of the process and vicariously savor the food. Were the seductive nature and persuasive communication techniques of those TV programs the reason why I have been an avid cook for the past thirty years? I wouldn't discount the idea.

People are rarely born with this ability. Most, chefs included, need to be taught how to speak this way and make it their default mode.

When I suggest storytelling, though, many clients tell me that they find it hard to incorporate more "antidotes" in their delivery. At first I'll try to reply using the correct word, *anecdote*. But when the hint isn't taken, I have to be a bit more overt and say, "I want you to add more anecdotes. An antidote is something you take if you've been poisoned or perhaps been forced to sit through a forty-slide PowerPoint presentation."

People mix up those two words all the time, even really smart people. It was this constant mixing up of the two words that made me realize that an anecdote is an exceptionally potent type of antidote, one that both cures and prevents one of the biggest diseases lurking in lecture halls, boardrooms, and even around the office watercooler: boredom.

PITCH-PERFECT POINTER

To understand the importance of visual storytelling, think back to when you were a kid. Did you ever tell stories around a campfire? Why do you think they were so riveting? I'll tell you: It was the vivid imagery that tickled your imagination. Now think about your high-school or college days and some of the lectures you sat through. Were many of your teachers and professors walking, breathing bottles of Ambien? Did they add greater weight to your eyelids with each abstract theory they droned on about? That's because they weren't telling stories. They were merely tossing out facts, figures, and information. The speakers who have kept you most engaged undoubtedly created verbal images that allowed you to see, hear, feel, and taste their message.

THE FORMULA FOR GREAT STORIES

So maybe you don't think you're a good storyteller. Perhaps you feel anecdotes don't come naturally to you. If you've told jokes in the past, only to have the punch lines land with a thud, the traumatic memory now probably puts a crimp in your storytelling style. The good news is that telling a good joke or story is a product of both nature and nurture. I suspect there's a certain genetic predisposition to having this quality (a 23andMe test can probably prove this), but using stories effectively to illustrate your points is a skill that can be acquired and strengthened.

Perhaps you've never had the components of a good story

broken down and analyzed before. If storytelling is not an innate talent, then for the time being, let's think of it as having a certain formula.

The Setup

Resist the urge to forecast or signpost. I have heard many presentations ruined by the speaker saying, "To illustrate this point, I'd like to share with you an anecdote." Does a Broadway actor stop in the middle of a scene to announce that a dramatic section of dialogue is coming up? Weave stories into your presentations, but don't make them feel like an appendage, an afterthought that got shoehorned in after the fact to an otherwise bland presentation.

The Build

Your build sets the scene, introduces key characters, and hints at some tension or conflict to be resolved. It also takes your listeners out of their heads and puts them inside yours, helping them to see exactly what you are visually describing. When formulating your build:

Don't assume your audience knows everything. Assuming that your listener already knows the who, where, and why is a quick way to kill a story. I call this the "curse of knowledge." It sets you up for stutter-stepping through the story with lines like, "Oh, wait a minute, I forgot to mention . . ." or "Actually come to think of it, this is important. To understand this story, you need to know . . ."

Try to keep the number of moving pieces in your narrative as few as possible. Your audience will get frustrated and tune out if they feel as though they need a flow chart to keep track of all the people in your story. Less is more in just about every form of communication. You'll learn more about this in chapter 5.

Make the build collapsible. If you have a lot of time, you can make it elaborate, with a number of twists and turns. If you are pressed for time or you sense your listeners are getting restless, you want to be able to omit much of the build, cutting sooner to the reveal. Your build should be so flexible that you can get in and out within fifteen seconds if needed.

No matter how long or short your build, you want it to create a sense of anticipation. Toward the end of the build, tease that the reveal is coming. This creates a drumroll effect, with your audience leaning in to hear what you are going to say next. A good tease might simply be:

"And then she did something totally out of character."
"And then something totally unexpected happened."
"And then she said something that won over everyone in the room."

The Reveal

This is the anecdotal equivalent of a joke's punch line. It's the payoff or the reward to your listener for staying attentive through the buildup. It's even more potent when it's counterintuitive, something your listener is not expecting. If you don't create an element of suspense and anticipation around the big reveal, your audience may miss it. The drumroll line serves as a warning to your listener to pay close attention at the most critical time.

The Exit

Once you deliver the reveal, let it sit there for a beat or two. Many people tell me that pausing makes them nervous. They worry that they'll lose the audience when they stop talking. Yet pausing creates the opposite effect. It allows your story to sink in and ensures that your audience can fully take in the meaning of what you've just told them.

HOW TO ADD SOME SCORSESE

It's the visual details that allow you to sit in the director's chair and dictate the images that your listener will be visualizing as you speak. Without them, you'll be confronted with a listener who, in the middle of your story, looks past your shoulder for social rescue, the international signal for "I'm bored." Once you know the setup, build, reveal, and exit for your story, it's time to add some Scorsese-like attention to detail.

PITCH-PERFECT POINTER

If you struggle with visual details, one of the following techniques might help.

THE STORYBOARD TECHNIQUE

Draw your story on a board, creating a new box and picture for each step forward in the story. If you can't think of something to draw in a given box, your story is missing needed visual details.

THE SCREENPLAY TECHNIQUE

Pretend everything you plan to say will be conveyed not through words but through moving images—like a movie. You don't narrate a movie like a book. You show it. Close your eyes and see if you can watch your story as if it were a film.

You might be tempted to think, *Some stories just aren't visual.* I don't believe that's true. I've worked with hundreds and hundreds of people over the years, helping them to add visual elements to countless stories. I have yet to meet a story that can't be told in a visual way.

Not long ago, an economist was in my office for media training. He wanted to make the point that countries like Brazil had improved their economies immensely in just thirty years. His inclination was to deliver the point as if he were in a Harvard Business School lecture hall: "When you look at a country like Brazil from a short-term historical perspective, the macro view you have is of a country that has transformed itself from one of enormous currency volatility and hyperinflation to one of stable growth."

One more sentence and you might be tempted to run off and make your own sandwich, right?

That's the kind of point that is begging for visual detail. It's also precisely the kind of point that many people assume can't be made visual.

Except it can.

I asked this client to describe what was going on in Brazil back in the 1980s.

"If you remember in Brazil thirty years ago, people were loading bags of suddenly worthless cash into wheelbarrows and carting them off to their local bank to trade them in for a mere walletful of the new currency the government had introduced that week . . . that's how bad inflation was. It was like showing up at a boutique with a dozen tattered and soiled evening dresses and hoping to exchange them for one new blouse," he said.

Now that's better. Visual anecdote + analogy ≠ boredom.

One good story deserves another, right? Last year I coached a coffee-bean adventure seeker—the kind of big personality you hope sits next to you at a dinner party. He would regale you all night with his tales of world travel into exotic and faraway locales in search of the best coffee beans he can find. That is his job, and if there's anybody who should be delivering a verbal screenplay, it's this guy. But even he, this Indiana Jones of the caffeine crowd, somehow lapsed into speaking in a theoretical and abstract way to make his points.

I asked him if he ever feels pressure when it comes time to sampling and tasting these newly discovered coffee beans. He said:

"Sure. I mean, you always want your instincts to be right because you've put a lot of resources into making this trip happen and sometimes the economic future of some village will be determined by what kind of assessment you make."

Not a bad answer, but there's nothing there to illustrate the sheer drama behind what he really does. For all I know, he could be some paper pusher sitting behind a desk reviewing loan applications to be branded with either an APPROVED or REJECTED stamp. To help him find a more visual way to tell a particular story about coffee, I asked him to describe a particular scene that could help me experience that moment-of-truth pressure vicariously. His response provided the goods I was looking for:

"When I come down off some mountain in a remote village where I've gathered a new source of coffee beans, there's usually this pivotal moment that takes place in the center of the village. All the villagers gather to see if this coffee bean is going to live up to its hype. They're all watching and waiting for my reaction, in fact they crowd around me, peering over my shoulder waiting for that thumbs-up, thumbs-down signal. At that moment, I am El Exigente."

HOW TO BE MARTIN SCORSESE WITH BEN BERNANKE CONTENT

What do the storytelling styles of a legendary Hollywood director have in common with those of a former chairman of the Federal Reserve Board? Absolutely nothing. That's why it can be so challenging to turn statistics and data into visual pictures. But if you don't rise to that challenge, you miss an opportunity to make your data as meaningful as possible.

So practice the art of the analogy. Consider the following:

- We've improved our efficiency 30 percent—that's like Michael Phelps shaving a minute off his swimming time in the 400-meter.
- Every year, fifty-six thousand women die from heart disease. Think of how many seats there are in the average baseball stadium. The victims of this disease would fill those stadiums beyond capacity.
- We've discovered an accounting error that is causing our company to lose $375,000 every single month. That's like a Ferrari dealer allowing one customer a month to test-drive a Testarossa and not bring it back. No way would that be tolerated.

Analogies do more than hold attention. They contextualize the data to help your listener understand it better. When you throw a number at your listeners, they don't know how to react to it. Is it a big number? A small number?

Your tone of voice can help too. If your statistic is surprising, raise your pitch to convey that feeling. If it's disappointing, let your audience know through a deeper tone that you find that unacceptable. For instance, let's say your company revenues were excellent in the previous quarter, so excellent that all managers will be seeing nice, fat bonuses. You want to convey *wow* as you say that number. So slow your pace down and pull down on your volume as you do so. This will boldface and underline your statistic even more.

Many of the same rules for brevity with words also apply to numbers: less is more. How vital is this stat? Don't include statistics just for the sake of fattening up your presentation with gratuitous data. Know why you are using each one—and use it well.

> ## PITCH-PERFECT POINTER
>
> If you have no other choice but to use a nonvisual statistic, then help your listener by stating it in two different ways. Numbers go by quickly, which means there's always the risk of your audience missing them. So find two different ways to make the same point, such as using a number and a percentage: "Our revenues are up five million dollars this quarter," and then just for emphasis follow with "that's an eighteen percent increase over last year."

PRACTICE YOUR SCORSESE

Don't tell your story for the first time during an important presentation. Try it out first at low-impact events: the dinner table and cocktail parties. Once you've told your story in several settings with much success, it's ready for prime time.

As you practice telling your story, pay attention to the body language of your listener. Your friends and family probably won't tell you if your story is boring them to oblivion, but their body language will. Consider the Six Clues That You've Lost Your Listener:

1. Fidgety Feet: Your listener just can't seem to stand still and is shifting position.
2. REM (Rapid Eye Movement): Your listener's eyes pinball all around the room to see if something more interesting might be happening elsewhere.
3. The Hand Windmill: Your listener waves his or her hand in a circular motion, indicating, "I get it, move on."
4. The Phone Check: Your listener looks at a device instead of at you.

5. The Shoulder Gaze: Rather than making eye contact, your listener gazes over your shoulder—to spot someone more interesting to talk to.
6. The Story Highjack: Your listener fills in your blanks and finishes your sentences just to bring the conversation to an earlier conclusion.

Sometimes we get so inside our own heads that we miss these cues. And while they may seem rude and annoying, they serve a useful purpose. Think of them as a barometer for how engaging you are and the level of skill you bring to storytelling. It will also help you to develop an important instinct: cutting to the punch line. Remember: your build is collapsible. When you notice someone showing one of the six clues, shrink the build as much as possible, cutting straight to your reveal.

The ability to quickly pivot to your reveal is essential. It may be the tool that prevents you from losing your audience. You have to be somewhat chameleonlike as a storyteller, because a story that one person finds compelling might feel long to another. Different people will also have different thresholds and tolerances for how long they will be invested in any story.

Use these tips to improve your storytelling even more:

Vary Your Delivery

Your voice has three tools: pitch (the tone, high or low), pace (the speed), and projection (the volume). Try to vary all three. When you want a key point to stick with your audience, slow your pace and deliver it more emphatically. Taking your time to convey this thought signals to your listener that it has greater importance. A brief pause after delivering a key point also allows the thought to sink in and resonate.

A few years back, when Steve Jobs was introducing the iPad,

he wanted his audience to know that Apple outshone all the competition. He somewhat rapidly gave them a few comparisons showing that Apple did more business than other large device manufacturers, such as Samsung, mentioning that Apple was now a $50-billion-a-year company. Then, to drive his point home, he dramatically slowed his pace as he said, "Apple is the number one . . . mobile devices company . . ." Then he paused. He waited for a beat before lowering his voice to a whisper, " . . . in the world."

Know Your Audience

Who are they? How do they like to consume their information? If you've got an audience of number crunchers, you can rely more heavily on data and less heavily on storytelling. If, on the other hand, you've got a more creative audience, then bar graphs are not a good approach.

Part of knowing your audience also relates to the Six Clues. The better you know your listeners, the more easily you can read their body language and the less likely it is that you will misinterpret them. Years ago, I worked with Jack Welch, the former chair of GE, a guy who certainly knows how to speak without filler or fluff. Frequently during meetings, he would give someone the "hand windmill"—waving it around in circles as if to say, "Will you cut to the chase already?" Unfortunately some people misconstrued Jack's windmill to mean "Give me more detail," which they would do until Jack finally couldn't take it anymore and would say, "No, I get it. Move on."

Providing TMNI (too much needless information) is one of the quickest ways to find yourself on the receiving end of the hand windmill. I've worked with people who are so sharp that I tell them something once very concisely and they say, "Yep, got it. Next?" before I'm even done with a sentence. They are the kind of people who want to squeeze eight hours of work into four, and you better not be the person standing in their way. Their time is valuable to them, and they don't appreciate its being wasted. When in doubt, err on the side of brevity.

Don't Assume Anything

Don't assume your political, religious, or personal opinions are the same as your listeners. When I show examples of speech blunders from politicians in my presentations, I try to be completely bipartisan. The rules of a dinner party apply to all work situations: indulging in discussions about sex, politics, or religion is like handling a loaded grenade.

Psych Yourself Up

If you truly believe your story merits telling and is interesting, you'll naturally deliver it with a greater sense of importance. But if that evil inner critic tells you, "I'm sure they've heard this before" or "They are going to hate this," then you'll likely deliver it with a sense of apology and defeatism. Your audience absorbs what you project.

Become the Most Brutal Editor You Know

Each time you tell the same story to a new audience, you create another opportunity to find places to trim it. Be on the lookout for boring, nonessential facts and jettison them. Does your listener really need to know that a house was blue or that the story took place five years ago? Keep details that make a story more interesting. Edit out details that are not important to understanding its significance.

Don't Sweat the Details

If it happened four years ago instead of five, don't correct yourself midsentence. If you get bogged down in such minute discrepancies as you tell a story, you'll lose your pacing and momentum.

As an example, read the following paragraph out loud. Record yourself as you do so. Then play the recording back. Where would you would lose attention?

> Five years ago my family took a trip to the Brazilian jungle. You know, I'm sorry, that trip was actually to Costa Rica; it wasn't Brazil. In any event, we were there as part of a school archaeology field trip. You know, now that I think about it, it was Brazil. Sorry. So . . . it was just me and my family and, oh yeah, my sister's boyfriend. I forgot he was there. And then during our final week, his cousin joined us, even though he kind of invited himself; I'm not sure anybody really wanted him there. Anyway, there we were walking through this jungle, and our tour guide, who was probably in his midthirties . . . I'm pretty sure that's how old he was because he said he graduated from some university in Argentina back in the early 2000s, so that would make him . . . yeah, that would make him certainly younger than forty. Although he's spent a lot of time in the sun, so he looks a little older than he might actually be. . . .

Cue the hand windmill!

It's more important to keep the story moving than it is to get every last tiny detail 100 percent accurate. Don't correct yourself or restate anything. Doing so only bogs down your story.

WHERE GREAT STORIES LURK

While storytelling may seem easier than conveying more abstract and theoretical content, never trick yourself into thinking that the formulation of good anecdotal material requires less effort. The night before a big speech or presentation, you never want to be racking your brain trying to come up with engaging stories.

A better strategy: pretend you are a novelist who is searching for stories all the time. Carry a notebook in your pocket or handbag. When interesting occurrences or conversations happen and the story symbolizes a point you frequently make in speeches, meetings, conversations, and interviews, write it down. If you don't, I guarantee you'll forget it.

Then whenever you need to weave a story into a presentation, check your notebook. If you do this, you'll find that you're never desperate for material. You'll always have a riveting way to illustrate your points and captivate your listeners every single time.

5

THE PASTA-SAUCE PRINCIPLE

A good speech should be a like a woman's skirt: long enough
to cover the subject and short enough to create interest.
— WINSTON CHURCHILL

LEARNED ABOUT THE connection between cooking and conversation at age sixteen when my mother asked me to leave football practice early and go with her to a cooking demonstration at Macy's in New York City.

Because I understood how much she wanted to go, I tried to summon a good attitude. Still, at that time in my life, I assumed that my passing skills as a quarterback would hold more sway with members of the opposite sex than my prowess in the kitchen. (Boy, was I ever wrong about that one!)

When we walked into Macy's, I fully expected to find some ladle-wielding, apron-clad hack hawking a cookbook. Instead, standing at the front of the room, towering over her kitchen assistant, was the first celebrity chef: Julia Child. With her breathy and enthusiastic delivery, she captivated me, and when the demonstration was over, I was first in line to buy her cookbook.

Now, years later, I love cooking as much as my mother did, and my dream assignments have been the ones that combine my profession with my passion: coaching famous chefs. From Thomas Keller to Marcus Samuelsson, and from Guy Fieri to Iron Chef Masaharu Morimoto, every single one has been an utter delight.

It was during these coaching sessions with chefs that I couldn't help but notice several incredible parallels between cooking and communicating. Two in particular stand out: less is more and simpler is better. In fact, good communication is a lot like pasta sauce. The more you boil down and reduce a sauce, the more dynamic the flavor. Speaking redundantly and using filler words in your communication is like adding water to the sauce. The result is something bland and forgettable.

FIVE REASONS NOT TO TALK LONGER

Ironically, the day I sat down to write this chapter, a woman came by the office to get some career advice. I wish I had been rolling a video or audio recorder to capture her relentless barrage of disjointed and disconnected thoughts. After spewing for close to five minutes, she finally invited my input. "What do you think it takes to be a successful media trainer?" I replied with just seventeen words: "You must be able to teach people to convey their most compelling thoughts as concisely as possible." She looked at me with an "Is that it, is that all?" expression.

Why do people go on too long, as this woman did? Usually they do it for one or more of the following reasons:

To Drive Home a Point

People think that the more they elaborate and explain, the more convincing they will be. They confuse quantity with persuasiveness. So they often say the same thing over and over again, talk in circles, and even tell random stories that don't support their message. This, however, doesn't persuade people. Instead, it bores them.

To Seem Smart

Abe Lincoln is alleged to have said, "Better to remain silent and be thought a fool than to speak out and remove all doubt." The more you talk, the more you risk proving Honest Abe right. In reality, the quietest person in any room is often the most intriguing, as well as the most powerful. By remaining quiet, the person creates more conversational open space, which invariably gets filled by others who are more uncomfortable with silence. You don't want to be the person filling the dead air. Strive to be the person in control.

To Take Up the Full Time That Was Allotted

One of the greatest gifts you can give your colleagues is the gift of time. Communicating efficiently may allow you to end a meeting or a lecture ten to fifteen minutes early and restore a bit of sanity to others' crazy work calendars. And for that, you may just become their personal hero.

Poor Planning

You've been given twenty minutes for your presentation. So how on earth could you still have ten slides to go but only two minutes left? Two possible explanations: you never timed yourself during a rehearsal, and/or you encouraged the audience to jump in and make it interactive but you didn't account for the fact that those interruptions chew up time. If you welcome audience participation, allow for one third of the time to be dedicated to that. If you are still running behind schedule, don't speed up your speaking pace or skip through entire slides. Both will make you look scattered and unprofessional. Instead scale back your information about each bullet in the slide to your most sparse explanation while maintaining a controlled, unhurried pace.

To Exploit a Captive Audience

Just because someone is sitting next to you on a plane doesn't mean you have the right to turn your seatmate into your personal sounding board. Don't assume that the other person:

- Wants to hear every little detail of your life.
- Doesn't have something else to do, such as get some work done, take a nap, or simply enjoy some peace and quiet.
- Specifically requested that seat assignment because you're such a fascinating person.

When I'm on a flight, I rarely offer any information about myself until the person next to me inquires. This is especially true if I sense that the conversation represents a possible business networking opportunity. In that case, the last thing I want to do is seem overly eager to sell and self-promote.

PITCH-PERFECT MAKEOVER

Recently on a flight home from San Francisco, the woman sitting next to me broke several CCRs (cardinal conversation rules). The first was answering my standard "How's it goin'?" question with a long-winded story about her life.

I found myself wishing that I:

(A) Had kept my blabbermouth-canceling headphones within reach, not stowed in the overhead.

(B) Could hand her a copy of the etiquette memo (which she clearly didn't get) warning of the dangers of TMI and that the only response anyone really wants to hear to my ice-breaking pleasantry is "Fine."

Unfortunately, because she needed some desperate communications help, the flight turned into a busman's holiday for me. I can't help it. I often end up listening to someone like that with a strict diagnostic ear, and she gave me plenty to diagnose (and material to jot down for this chapter).

WHAT SHE SAID

"So, yeah, this has been a real drag with my son. He broke his arm in a big lacrosse game to determine the regional champions. So he missed most of the game since the injury happened early in the game, in fact it was kind of on a dirty play where this kid on the other team whacked him with his stick. My husband was so incensed that he practically had to be restrained from running onto the field and complaining to the referees. He has a history of that, my husband. It goes all the way back to Little League. The umpires were always pointing to him in the stands and warning him to be quiet or they'd eject him. So of course now we're worried that this injury will ruin our son's chances of getting a lacrosse scholarship because this is the time of year when the scouts are out in full force . . . and being the teenager he is, everyone in the family is subjected to his moodiness over the fact that he can't play. . . ."

HOW SHE COULD HAVE CONDENSED IT:

"If any of your children are high-school athletes, I'm sure you get wrapped up in how their season is going. Well, right now the mood is pretty low in our house. My son broke his arm during a big lacrosse game the other day, right when college scouts are taking a close look at whom to offer scholarships to. So we've had to figure out a plan B and somehow keep his spirits up."

HOW TO BOIL DOWN A MESSAGE

If you struggle with the whole notion of brevity, it might be useful to think of words like calories. Every day you have a set number to play with, let's say two thousand. Exceeding that amount never leads to anything good. From my front-row seat watching and analyzing how people communicate, I can tell you that there is a verbal obesity epidemic. I'm sure you've witnessed it yourself. Have you ever stood by helplessly while someone engaged in binge talking?

People take far too long to make their point, and even after they do, they tend to drone on repetitively. If we were all put on a verbal diet, I bet we'd make what we say really matter and become more effective communicators.

Another major incentive to subscribe to brevity has to do with the attention span of audiences—it's disappearing faster than the polar ice caps. E-mails are now considered long and cumbersome compared to the much-preferred text. Tweets trump blog posts. That's just the world we live in. So if our listeners are capable of digesting only smaller helpings of information, why do we think that serving them family-size portions will work?

Your communication should leave people feeling satisfied, not stuffed and bloated.

Being concise is hard to do. It takes practice. If you struggle to boil things down, try this:

Develop Decisive Starts and Finishes

Know your opening—the first sixty to ninety seconds of content that will come out of your mouth—and have it down cold. That's when you're going to be the most nervous, so leave nothing to chance. Once you're out of the starting blocks cleanly and smoothly, your confidence will build. The same holds true for your close. It should be a definitive destination you're driving to with a sense of purpose. Make it firm and give it a little punch. What I tend to hear more often are wishy-washy rehashes and synopses that coast to the finish line rather than sprint. The middle of your presentation, however, should be expandable or collapsible, so it can grow or shrink, depending on time constraints and how your audience is receiving it.

I'm not talking about being able to shrink your presentation by a minute or two. I'm talking about being able to cut it by a third or even by half. It happens more often than you might think. While in Zurich training a number of female executives recently, I learned that the company had designated only thirty minutes for what I'd thought was going to be an hour-long presentation. I had just ten minutes to find a way to boil the talk down. I did it by removing twelve of the thirty slides in the middle of the talk.

If you're ever called upon to do the same sort of on-the-spot reduction, do the following:

- Maintain your original headline, whether it be a story, startling statement, or unusual statistic. You've practiced this. Don't mess with it.
- Slice from the middle. For instance, if the middle of your talk has five points, cut out points two and three.
- Now you'll need some segues. Think about ways to conversationally connect point one to point four.
- Then make sure the newer, shorter talk still builds to the same ending that you've practiced.

Sever Your Emotional Ties to the Content

Rarely do I come across a client's presentation that isn't improved by cutting it by about 25 percent. Don't fall so deeply in love with your own content that you can't see that some of it is excess. I guarantee that your audience will not miss all the elements that were in the original version (and as I mentioned above, they'll thank you for your brevity!). By cutting, you'll be honoring the contemporary horror author Stephen King, who wrote in his memoir *On Writing*, "Kill your darlings, kill your darlings, kill your darlings, even when it breaks your egocentric little scribbler's heart, kill your darlings." It's a horrible expression, but while sacrificing something you've created and feel attached to can be gut-wrenching, the content only becomes stronger.

Use the Headline Principle

Get to your point immediately. Don't slowly build up to it.

Practice, Practice, Practice

Time yourself each time, continually shrinking your delivery until you've got your message boiled down to its most flavorful essence. As I suggested with the Scorsese Principle, practice in front of others and be on high alert for the Six Clues That You've Lost Your Listener (page 73).

Don't Commit to a Number

Do you remember the moment Rick Perry lost his bid for the 2012 Republican nomination for president? It was when he said he would eliminate three departments from the US government, but he could remember only two of them. Forecasting exactly how many points you are going to make is riskier than leaving it more general with "several" or "a few."

Always Leave Them Wanting More

Don't succumb to the overused technique of recapping or summarizing everything you just said. Nothing makes people sink down into their chairs more than the line, "So let me just quickly recap what we just went over." Instead, at the end of your presentation, suggest they try something new, or adopt a new strategy or way of thinking, and then project the future benefits they'll reap if they heed your advice. To end one of my talks on how to give a speech, I said, "So the next time you give a speech, think about starting with content that's unpredictable, visual, and anecdotal. I think you will find your audience is more engaged and your message resonates more effectively."

FOUR CONVERSATIONAL SAUCES THAT TASTE BETTER WHEN CONDENSED

Do you have to boil down every single message? It's not a bad idea, but there are some situations when a flavorful, condensed message is much more important than others. Use these recipes for the following speaking situations.

Delivering a Speech

As I've mentioned, attention begins wavering eighteen minutes into a lecture. Some research also shows that you have to be pretty skilled to hold them through the full eighteen minutes. Usually attention drops off even sooner, with people losing their focus just five minutes in, tuning in and tuning back out frequently afterward. As a result, time your message so it stays within the eighteen-minute limit. Practice your talk ahead of time so you know exactly how long it lasts—and remove slides and points until you've got your talk boiled down to eighteen minutes or fewer. Also create mini three-to-five-minute segments within your talk. That way you'll be transitioning to a new topic before your audience loses focus.

Answering a Question

I realize that one often-recommended strategy calls for not relinquishing the floor once you have it. But panel participation is not football: the player with the longest time of possession doesn't necessarily win. Follow the Headline Principle and devise a provocative and punchy statement for each of the topic areas the moderator will raise. Then illustrate your point with an example, a story or some compelling data—or maybe a combination of the three—and then button it with a line or two reaffirming your main point but framing it differently than your headline. Then relinquish the floor.

Pitching a New Client

The magic ratio here is roughly three to one. The amount of time you dedicate to listening to your clients and discussing their challenges should be three times what you spend talking about yourself. The key strategy here is to play a match game. Identify what the new client needs most to achieve his or her goals. Then find a successful case study to show you've provided something similar. The extent of your pitch could be merely, "A few months ago, we helped one of our clients through a situation very similar to what you're going through. Fortunately, the issue is resolved and they're back on track. So if you ever want us to give you a hand with that, just shout. It's something we're very familiar with." In just four short sentences you:

1. Establish that you have recent experience performing the kind of work they need.

2. Give them a peek around the corner to a good outcome.

3. Offer your services, but not in a pushy, desperate way. Rather it's a let-them-come-to-you way.

4. Show that the kind of work they need is aligned with your professional sweet spot.

Making Small Talk During a Work Function

I'm amazed by how much time people spend whining and complaining about their kids, weekend plans that went awry, their aging and infirm parents, and of course, the boss. The standard question "How's it going?" should not unleash a fire hose of negativity. I'll let you in on a little secret: in posing the question, your work colleague is really interested in only one response: "Pretty good! How about you?" Small talk should be just that: small. I think we're under some delusion that bitching and moaning about work is the glue that holds us together as colleagues. Ultimately, though, it's corrosive to a culture and just makes the workplace worse. If you're miserable at work, you have two choices: work to fix what's wrong with the place or leave. Bringing as many people down with you as you can is not a third option.

I could keep going, giving you dozens of ways to condense all sorts of messages, but something tells me that doing so would counter the very point I'm trying to make. Plus, the best way to master the Pasta-Sauce Principle isn't memorizing a list of tips. It's this: paying attention to your words as well as the words of others. Do that and I think you'll find that much of what you and others say just isn't necessary, and that every point could be made better and clearer with fewer words rather than more.

6

THE NO-TAILGATING PRINCIPLE

. . . no word was ever as effective as a rightly timed pause.
—MARK TWAIN

IF THE 24/7 cable news landscape has taught us anything, it's this: if you want to dominate a conversation, don't come up for air. In the news equivalent of the pro wrestling ring, he who takes a millisecond to breathe loses the floor. You could call it the Chris Matthews doctrine. This fire-hose approach to communicating has gotten the rest of us into some pretty bad habits.

Many people try to maintain an uninterrupted stream of sound coming from their mouths, worrying that clients, colleagues, and supervisors will interpret the slightest pause as a sign of uncertainty. And let's face it, most of us are just plain uncomfortable with the whole notion of silence. As a result, we talk quickly and nonstop, especially when trying to keep the floor, seem more energetic, or win an argument.

We end up accomplishing the opposite.

The more quickly we talk, the more likely we are to put people to sleep, sacrifice our credibility, or worst of all, accidentally say something we'll regret. Think of your brain and your mouth as two cars traveling down a road. The brain is the lead car and the mouth is drafting a millisecond right behind, conversationally steering in the direction the brain tells it to go. At any given moment, the brain is choosing which verbal road to travel and the exact words needed to articulate each thought.

The more slowly you drive the rear car (your mouth), the more time you give your brain to carefully decide where the mouth is going to go next. Likewise, your mouth has more time to smoothly turn in any given conversational direction the brain tells it to go. It's exactly like following a friend who is driving in a separate car in front of you. The more time you give each other to prepare to turn or stop, the smoother and less dangerous the maneuver will be.

The object is to keep your mouth a safe car length from your brain. The more quickly you talk, however, the closer the mouth travels to the brain. I call this verbal tailgating. When this happens, the brain doesn't have enough time to make careful and thoughtful decisions. End result: the brain is forced into choosing the first direction (or thought) rather than the best one. This is why we often find ourselves in a conversational dead end, saying something irrelevant or, worse, inappropriate. Ask anyone who has said something regrettable, "What on earth possessed you to say that?" and the answer will probably be, "I don't know, I just kind of said the first thing that popped into my head." That's probably what happened to the Danish film director Lars von Trier at the Cannes Film Festival in 2011. During a routine press conference about his film *Melancholia*, he was asked a question about his German roots. In one long and winding answer, he said, "I found out that I was really a Nazi because my family was German, which also gave me some pleasure. What can I say? I understand Hitler. But I think he did some wrong things. Yes, absolutely, but I can see him sitting in his bunker in the end. . . . He's not what you would call a good guy, but, yeah, I understand much about him and I sympathize with him a little bit. I am not for the Second World War, but . . . I am, of course, very much for Jews. No, not too much, because the Israelites are a pain in the ass. . . ."

Kirsten Dunst, one of the stars of his film, was sitting next to him and looked on in horror, probably weighing the risks and rewards of just getting up and leaving.

Realizing how deeply he had strayed into toxic territory, von Trier then verbalized what most of us just think: "How can I get out of this sentence?"

The interviewer replied, "By another question. Here's your salvation."

It's rare for a journalist to offer a life preserver like that. Usually they just let you hang in your noose a bit longer until they hear your neck snap. To be more thoughtful and selective, we need time. To gain more time, we need to slow down. Yes, it really is as simple as that.

Speaking fast is a high-risk proposition. It's nearly impossible to maintain the ideal conditions to be persuasive, articulate, and effective when the mouth is traveling well over the speed limit. Although we'd like to think that our minds are sharp enough to always make good decisions with the utmost efficiency, they just aren't. In reality, the brain arrives at an intersection of four or five possible things to say and sits idling for a couple of seconds, mulling over the options. When the brain stops sending navigational instructions back to the mouth and the mouth is moving too fast to pause, that's when you get a verbal fender bender, otherwise known as filler. *Um, ah, you know,* and *like* are what your mouth does when it has nowhere to go.

YOU MIGHT BE A VERBAL TAILGATER IF

- The first six words out of your mouth are "Well, you know, I think that . . ."
- Your audience is left wondering what your main point was.
- It takes you two or three times as long to make a point as people who are more concise.

- You rely too heavily on *um*, *ah*, or other filler.
- You can't be certain what you're likely to say five to ten words down the road.
- You often find yourself saying, "How did I get off on that tangent?" and "How do I get home from here?"

YOU CAN'T FIX A FENDER BENDER

Verbal fender benders can certainly take a toll. For instance, not long ago a client from a fairly straitlaced company told me this story about an up-and-coming managing director. The executive was chatting with the company's CEO during a cocktail party. She was understandably nervous, and her jitters had a predictable effect on her. Her nerves accelerated her speaking pace. She lost control, allowing an F-bomb to slip from her mouth. That one crucial error created a shift in perception from "up-and-coming" to "loose cannon."

Unlike a vehicular fender bender, there aren't any repair shops for your reputation and professional image. Technological advancements, of course, trick us into thinking that we can clean up a verbal wreck. Our mouths don't come equipped with UNDO and DELETE buttons, but our computers do. We can post something on Facebook and, after the fact, limit who sees it through the privacy settings, but similar drop-down menus don't exist in real life. If you've ever said something you wish you could take back, then you know what I mean. For anyone in the public eye, the seven most dreaded words to have to utter are either "What I really meant to say was . . ." or "No way was I trying to imply . . ."

It's never more important to slow down or pause than when you are in unfamiliar territory. Ad-libbing or attempting for spontaneity is like driving on a foggy mountain road where you can't see more than six inches beyond the hood of the car. You have no idea what danger lurks around the next bend. Worse yet, you don't even know where the bends are in the road! That's why I suggest you severely curtail ad-libbing, especially during high-stakes communication situations. (See Chapter 10 for more.)

Former BP chairman Tony Hayward knows this all too well. During the catastrophic oil spill in the Gulf of Mexico in 2010, he agreed to answer reporters' questions in an attempt to show his genuine concern for the growing crisis. He was spouting off his memorized corporate talking points. Seemingly all was going according to plan. Then Hayward decided to add an extra little something to the end of his vetted key messages, something that he might have thought made him more relatable to the blue-collar workers whose businesses his faulty oil well was destroying. He said, "There's no one who wants this thing over more than I do. You know, I'd like my life back."

Ka-boom! The media replayed his comment on every news talk show, and within months, Hayward was shown the door at BP.

Hayward made such a critical mistake for two reasons:

1. He fooled himself into thinking he was on a roll. He probably thought, *Let me go for a little more by adding something personal.*
2. His extra content was ad-libbed. It had to have been, because if any of his handlers had ever heard him say it before, they certainly would have warned him. "You know you can't say something like that to a reporter, right?"

If Hayward had the luxury of an UNDO button, here is how I would advise him to say it differently: "All of my non-company-related plans have been put on hold until I am personally satisfied with where we are in resolving this crisis. What's happening in the Gulf deserves my full attention, and it has my full attention, along with that of the most talented and knowledgeable people we have, who are working around the clock to find answers and solutions to this terrible situation."

It's easy to poke fun at Hayward's and other people's verbal fender benders, yet most people—without the presence of mind to slow down and pause—would get into a similar wreck in the same situation.

WHY YOU TAILGATE

Certain situations encourage Verbal Tailgating. They include:

Being on the Defensive

Many people think that the faster they talk, the more convincing they'll sound. As I've said before, however, the opposite is true. The more quickly you talk, the more defensive, anxious, and uncertain you sound.

Anxiety

Whenever you are tense and anxious, your thoughts speed up, triggering you to accelerate your speaking pace, too. The more adrenaline you have, the faster you will be tempted to talk, and the more verbal fender benders you'll have along the way.

Discomfort

Many of us are uncomfortable with silence, so we compensate by filling that silence with words.

Intelligence

It's possible that highly intelligent people simultaneously contemplate more thoughts more quickly than the non-Mensa crowd. This can be a handicap when it comes to public speaking, one I like to call the curse of the intelligentsia. The brains of highly intelligent people tend to speed far ahead of their mouths. While their mouths are articulating one thought, their brains, already bored, are now two thoughts ahead. As a result, highly intelligent people often interrupt themselves, not finishing one thought before quickly moving on to an unrelated one. They end up sounding scattered and disjointed—not an accurate reflection of how intelligent they really are.

Mirroring

If you are conversing with a fast talker, you might be tempted to mirror that person and speed up your own pace, too. I see this a lot with guests on CNN's Headline News show *Nancy Grace* or with people who are being interviewed by shock jocks. Rather than patiently wait for an opening and speak at their own pace, they get swept into the manic nature of the conversation.

Competition

If you are at a pitch meeting or brainstorming session, you might speak quickly without a hint of a pause for fear that you will lose the floor. In reality, the more slowly you talk and the shorter and more targeted your message, the less likely it is that someone will interrupt you. Droning on excessively is how you conversationally overstay your welcome.

FIVE COMPELLING REASONS TO STOP TAILGATING

In addition to avoiding career-wrecking moments, slowing down and pausing between thoughts will help you to:

Hold Attention

Your listener craves a discernible structure to what you're telling them, complete with a beginning, middle, and end. When the ear registers one steady, unbroken stream of chatter, it gets overwhelmed and gives up. I often equate this to how you feed a baby. Give a small spoonful and then let the baby chew and swallow before you start shoveling in more. Try to accomplish too much too quickly, and the recipient rejects it. For a baby, that means spitting up. For a member of your audience, that means tuning out.

It's for this reason that consumers are more likely to pay attention to a commercial with a silent segment. It's also why comedians come to a dead halt before delivering a punch line. The silence attracts attention, giving the next thought more impact.

Exude Confidence

Confident people characteristically take things slowly, firm in their belief that there's no need to rush because every single word they say matters.

To be an effective speaker, you must absolutely psych yourself up to think that you are imparting tremendous value to your listeners. The faster you talk, the more apologetic you sound, as if you are conveying your lack of worthiness to be taking up your audience's valuable time. One of the worst examples of this is an expression I hear all the time in corporate presentations, "Let me just quickly walk you through this." It's as if you're saying, "I know you're going to be bored stiff by this, but I have to cover it nonetheless." You would be better off saying, "OK, quick recap. Here's where we were this time last year. . . . This is where we are now." The more slowly you talk, using an economy of words, the more confident and sure of your message you appear.

Part with Your Verbal Eraser

A slower pace makes you less likely to resort to what I call verbal backspacing, saying things like, "Oh, I didn't really mean to say that. What I meant to say was this." To illustrate this notion, I will sometimes show clients a clip of Alicia Silverstone giving a presentation for her book *The Kind Diet*. The first thirty seconds are riddled with verbal backspacing: "So I . . . well . . . this book is . . . Well, thank you all for coming. . . . Or . . . thanks for having me here. I'm really honored to be here, . . . and I'm really, really . . ." Then she trails off as she leaves the podium and goes out of the camera shot for about five seconds to retrieve a glass of water.

Constantly searching for a better way to articulate a thought while you're in the middle of expressing it creates a halting and uncertain delivery that saps you of confidence and conviction. Whenever you feel the urge to verbally backspace, pause and relax into the notion that the first way you said it is now the best way.

Seem More Engaged

Whenever you are having a conversation, your mind should be working on parallel tracks: first and foremost, listening with genuine interest to the other person and, second, thinking what stories from your own personal experience meld nicely with the subject at hand. Pausing thoughtfully after the other person has completed a thought signals that you've heard what they've had to say, digested it, considered it, and are now basing your next contribution on what's just been said, rather than careening off with a non sequitur.

Your response will likely seem more genuine, sincere, engaged, and targeted.

Speak without Fillers—Naturally

As a communications coach, I probably get asked for help in this area more than any other, because professionals realize that removing the junk and fillers from their speech greatly enhances their image. Filler strips the conviction from our speech. Testimony by government officials before congressional committees offer numerous examples of the importance of not having filler be the first sounds you make. In October 2013, an official from the Department of Health and Human Services was asked during a congressional hearing whether the government knew in advance that the problem-plagued website health.gov would not be fully ready in time for its launch. The official started her answer with, "Um . . . uh." Regardless of how strong her answer went on to be, the uncertainty conveyed by that filler at the beginning called the accuracy of her answer into question.

Filler words are also a surefire way to annoy your listener. In a Marist Poll, for instance, survey respondents rated the following words and phrases as most annoying: *whatever, like, you know what I mean, to tell you the truth, actually, you know, it is what it is, anyway,* and *at the end of the day.*

I'm sure you've read or been told to omit these words from your speech. How's that working for you? For most people, it's not working so effectively, as one in every twenty words are fillers. Telling someone to stop saying *um, ah, like,* and *actually* is like telling a worrier to stop biting his nails. Calling attention to your filler words only creates anxiety, which can cause you to say more filler words. This is where slowing down and pausing can really help.

HOW TO MAINTAIN A SAFE TALKING DISTANCE

You probably think you talk more slowly and pause more often than you really do. Many people, for instance, tell me that the amount of time it takes them to take a sip of water in the middle of a presentation seems interminable. In reality, it's not that long at all. Similarly, the moment just after someone is asked a question feels quite long to most people, causing them to start talking before they've composed their thoughts. In reality, it felt long only in *their* minds.

It's for this reason that I encourage you to record yourself. A recording will give you an accurate measure of your vocal pace. It will also help you to hear your fillers, verbal backspacing, and other foibles. Awareness of the problem's existence is the first step to conquering it.

Modern technology makes recording yourself quite easy. You can use a webcam, a tablet, or a smartphone. You can even call someone on Skype and record yourself as you have a normal conversation.

When you play back the recording, take notice of:

- Filler words
- Verbal fender benders
- Verbal backspacing
- Tangents, repetitions, and lost trains of thought

Don't use your recording to beat yourself up. Use it just to get a sense of the extent of the problem and also as a way to gauge your progress. As you work on improving your delivery, use these pointers.

Mix Up Your Pace

Feel the freedom to briskly deliver thoughts that are quite familiar to you (ones you've said repeatedly to others) and then slow down to drive home your most important points or content that is less familiar to you.

Talk Cleanly

In the food industry, there's been a lot of discussion of the notion of clean eating: consuming basic, real ingredients instead of the multisyllabic, chemical-sounding, impossible-to-pronounce ones that permeate processed food. A concept I call clean talking is similar. The idea is to eliminate all the obscure jargon, the filler, the showoff vocabulary, and the complex, flowery, verbose sentence structure. Keeping it simple, straightforward, and clean (and delivering it at a moderate pace) gives your brain enough time to sort out the next thought, allowing you to progress from one idea to the next in an orderly, focused, and persuasive manner. You'll be a lot less likely to get ahead of yourself, forget important points, interrupt your own stream of thought, accidentally present your ideas in an illogical order, or go off on tangents.

Speaking cleanly is a very Zen experience. It's about being 100 percent focused on the thought you are in the midst of articulating. If you're talking away but your brain is replaying and analyzing something that you said five seconds ago because you're not sure it was the best way to say it, that puts you in peril. Allowing your mouth to continue without guidance from your brain could cause a whole host of problems.

When in Doubt, Stop Talking

The more uncertain you are about your next words, the more slowly you should speak, even coming to a dead stop if needed. Barack Obama frequently does this. When he arrives at a conversational intersection and realizes that his next word could have an enormous impact, he stops speaking for a beat or two until he is sure that the next word or sentence is his best choice. He rarely allows his speaking pace to pressure his brain into making a bad decision.

If you were an expert slot car driver growing up, then this discipline will be easy to grasp. With those toy cars, the key to being a good driver is to vary your speeds: fast on the straightaway sections of track and slow on the sharp curves. We tend to have two sections of mental track during conversation: content we feel confident in conveying (the straightaways) and thoughts that feel less practiced and more spontaneous, with uncertain word selection (the sharp curves). If you imagine yourself driving around that track and slowing down for the bends, filler words will be less likely to infiltrate your speech.

Focus on What You Want to Say,
Not on What You Think the Audience Is Thinking

Many people pay too much attention to how others perceive them, and this puts too much power in the hands of the listener and not enough in the head of the speaker. There is not enough bandwidth in your brain for you to concentrate simultaneously on your point, your delivery, and what you think your listener might be thinking based on his or her facial expressions. Guessing the engagement level of your audience will create excess anxiety that speeds up your pace. In reality, you can never know what's going on in someone else's head. Facial expressions aren't a referendum on your performance.

Listen More, Talk Less

Listening is one of the most effective compliments we have to offer. It validates others and makes them feel supported, and it also gives us a chance to thoughtfully prepare what we want to say. Attentive listening is becoming an increasingly rare commodity, which is why it is so easy to stand out and make a great impression by demonstrating that the art is not lost on you.

7

THE CONVICTION PRINCIPLE

. . . state your position with utter conviction, as the French
do, and you'll have a marvelous time!

—JULIA CHILD

BACK IN FIFTH grade, I had an English teacher named Bosworth Farson. His name evokes the image of a man in a tweed jacket and an ascot who is speaking through a pretentious prep-school lockjaw. Bo was nothing like that. He was supercool and handsome: a twenty-five-year-old rookie teacher in bell-bottoms (yes, they were cool back then) who loved jazz and rock 'n' roll and who insisted, among other things, that we read our compositions aloud at the front of the classroom.

As you might expect, we read these assignments with about as much grace as the Bad News Bears played baseball. There was a relentless shuffling of feet. Most of us mumbled our way through the content. Students trailed off at the end of sentences, with the last few words barely audible. Eyes remained glued to the paper the entire time.

Every week, one of my classmates in particular left no doubt as to the level of his performance anxiety and lack of conviction. He would start by saying, "Well, the first part stinks, and you probably don't want to hear the rest."

Of course, when you're eleven years old, that's the norm. Yet many adults lack as much conviction as my classmates and I did back in fifth grade. Their tone of voice, demeanor, and phrasing ranges from a slight tone of apology to full-blown defeatism, and it creeps into their presentations, pitches, and meetings.

When you speak, you want to sound filled with relentless conviction, exuding enthusiasm for the value of the information you're sharing. Your words, eye movement, posture, pitch, and tone of voice must convey certainty.

But demonstrating unshakable self-confidence is a process, especially if deep down you're feeling anything but. I often tell clients there are three stages of public speaking:

Stage 1: Dread

Stage 2: Tolerance

Stage 3: Enjoyment

When you're mired in dread, it seems as though stage three is some mythical fairyland that doesn't really exist. Very few people manage to leapfrog from number one to number three instantly. But if you're dedicated, you can gradually migrate from dreading it to tolerating it and then eventually to deriving an enjoyable buzz from it. It's like golf. If you learn sound mechanics from a pro and then go out and play frequently, you will play better and have more fun.

What I want to do for you in this chapter is to give you some good speaking mechanics that will help you mask your sense of dread from your audience. Just because you may be starting in stage one doesn't mean your audience has to know that. The trick is to simulate your sense of enjoyment until you can actually experience it for real.

SIX PHRASES OF EQUIVOCATION

One surefire way to undermine your sense of conviction is to use equivocating, wishy-washy phrases. These phrases are a way of not fully committing to your thoughts, ideas, and opinions. People mistakenly think that equivocation is a way of playing it safe, that by not demonstrating absolute certainty, they leave themselves less vulnerable to challenge and disagreement from their audience. Watering down your conviction, though, signals to your listener, *This is a weak idea.*

"Kind of" and "Sort of"

These two phrases pervade modern speech. I hear them frequently in business settings and elsewhere. They are a ubiquitous verbal tic, one of which few people are even aware.

Many of my clients use these as a way to safeguard against sounding opinionated or arrogant. But these words round off the edges of your thoughts, making your presentation tepid and your tone uncertain.

Consider the following examples:

"It was kind of successful" versus "It was a big hit."

"It's sort of what makes us distinctive" versus "It's what sets us apart."

"This is kind of what we're thinking" versus "This is what we have in mind."

In my experience as a coach, I have found women more susceptible to letting these words creep into their vocabulary than men are. Many women tell me of their struggles to find a harmonious middle ground between exuding gravitas and coming across too aggressive. I tell them that I would rather they soften their image by displaying a warm and friendly demeanor than by allowing this lukewarm language to take hold.

"I Think . . ."

Like *kind of*, this phrase is used to soften the blow of an opinion, but it just strips the conviction from your point. Consider the differences in the following:

"I think we should consider possibly changing our policy on this" versus "We should reexamine our policy."

"I think this is the way to go" versus "This is definitely the way to go."

"I think our priorities might need some rethinking" versus "Let's take a long, hard look at our priorities."

"You May Not Like This, but . . ."

Stay away from self-fulfilling prophecy. A clause like this forewarns your listeners that your idea will be unpopular but you are going to present it anyway. Starting with negativity causes your audience to frown on your idea before you've ever voiced it. Here are other similar phrases:

- "This is probably a dumb idea, but . . ."
- "I'm sure someone else will come up with something better, but . . ."
- "I don't know. It's probably not worth considering, but for the sake of brainstorming, how about . . ."

"Let Me Just Quickly . . ."

I mentioned this phrase when telling you about the Headline Principle. People use it when they suspect the information they're providing is completely obvious or redundant. These words usually come before "housekeeping" items, agenda setting, or a recap. If you feel you must "quickly" go through something, consider not going through it at all. If it's information your listener needs to know, don't apologize. Instead of "Let me just quickly walk you through our results from last quarter," try "Here's a snapshot of Q1."

"I'll Only Take Up Two Minutes of Your Time"

Next to "The check's in the mail," this is one of the most common lies of all. You often hear salespeople lead with this during cold calls and networking events, right before they ramble on for another fifteen minutes at least. They mistakenly think it's a good tactic because most people would be too ashamed to claim they don't have two measly minutes to give, so they oblige you. Do you really want to convey to the other person that you're only worth two minutes? Try saying, "I know we're both juggling crazy schedules, so I'll get right to the point."

It might take some discipline to extract these phrases from your speech. The first step is awareness. Pick one phrase a month to eliminate. Then pay attention to your speech throughout the day, trying to notice when you use the phrase. Whenever you feel tempted to equivocate, remember the Pasta Sauce and Tailgating principles. Say less. Slow way down. Insert a pause in the place you would normally use the word or phrase you are trying not to say. It's similar to the awareness nutritionists ask their clients to embrace every time there's food present—be thoughtful about everything you put *in* your mouth. Here, I'm suggesting you be aware of everything coming *out* of your mouth.

DON'T COPY YOUR COLLEAGUES

One of the worst ways to practice the Conviction Principle? Watch what many of your colleagues do, and then try to emulate them.

Three bad speaking habits pervade much of the business world, causing some of the most confident people to sound shaky and unsure of themselves:

Clichés

In a recent poll, Britons chose the insipid expression "at the end of the day" as the number one cliché infecting the king's English. Other culprits lurking very close behind are "leveling the playing field," "from this perspective/standpoint," and "let's walk through . . ." Another cliché that has infected every corporation in America is referring to a problem as a "challenge" or, worse yet, declaring that "we don't see this so much as a challenge, but rather an opportunity." It's the same with *journey*. How many times have you sat in a presentation and heard "We've only begun this journey . . ." or "As we embark on this journey to profitability . . ."

Industryspeak

Every industry has its jargon—words and phrases that everyone uses but hardly anyone truly understands. Recently when I was training an executive at an accessory fashion company, I asked her what goes into designing a new handbag. She answered, "Everything from the color to the fabrications." I couldn't help but ask, "What's a fabrication? In my book, a fabrication is a lie." Not only had this industry made up a word that does not resonate with consumers and is needlessly more complicated than *fabric*, but also it chose a word that is synonymous with lying. Anyone who gags at the notion of eating GMOs (genetically modified organisms) should find equally abhorrent the notion of speaking with JMWs (jargon-modified words).

If you had told someone twenty years ago that "putting your resources against your priorities" was anything other than self-sabotage, they would have thought you were crazy. That would have been just as nutty as the notion that "being disruptive" was something to be rewarded rather than punished. Who knows how far this transformation of the pejorative into the honorific will go? I'm actually thinking of pioneering my own definition flip-flopping. Perhaps pesky start-up companies will not just be disruptive to an entire industry, but also "iconoclastic" to the big well-established brands they're competing against. And their leaders' single-minded focus on achieving the company goals will be admiringly referred to as "petulance." It has a nice ring to it, don't you think?

It saddens me that this kind of corporate gobbledygook is so shockingly commonplace. We've all heard industryspeak since our very first days in business. We mistakenly think that by mimicking it, we'll fit into our corporate culture, just as those IBM guys in the 1970s all wore dark suits, white shirts, and sedate neckties to blend in.

I've had clients say, "I'm worried that if I don't use that jargon, my colleagues will think I don't know what I'm talking about." This notion couldn't be any more backward. Using meaningless corporatespeak is a crutch that obstructs the true depth of your knowledge. As Albert Einstein once allegedly said, "If you can't explain it simply, you don't understand it well enough."

To kick the jargon habit, try this. Practice your next presentation out loud using the recording device on your smartphone. Then take the audio content and have it transcribed. You see all those red lines under words like *efforting*, *choiceful*, and *incentivization*. That's a gentle reminder from your computer that you are using a made-up word. If it's not real, you shouldn't be using it.

Oversimplification

The opposite of industryspeak is what many people call "dumbing it down." How many times have you been implored to dumb something down so as to not lose the focus and attention of your audience? I'm all in favor of keeping communications simple and straightforward, but I've seen too many videos of people who think they're great communicators talking to people as though they're four-year-olds. Such verbal pabulum is downright offensive.

PITCH-PERFECT MAKEOVER

When I coached an executive from a beauty company, he was about to give a presentation to the sales force. His goal: to get them to buy into a new analytics tool his company was using to gauge what their customers wanted.

WHAT HE PLANNED TO SAY

"Good morning. I'm here to talk to you today about some new initiatives the brand has launched with regards to consumer insight. We're leveraging these efforts against understanding what our core consumer considers desirable and aspirational. To these ends, we recently engaged for the first time in a thorough questioning of our consumers resulting in extensive data which we believe will provide us best-in-class insights and allow us to better deliver against her needs."

WHAT I COACHED HIM TO SAY

"Think back to the best gift you've ever given someone, a gift that was perfectly suited to the recipient, utterly responsive to what was personally meaningful to that person. Such a gift hits the bull's-eye of personal taste so cleanly that we count the days till giving it because we can't wait to see the expression on the person's face. Now think of a gift you've given in the past that was one of sheer obligation—the "let's stop and pick something up because we can't arrive empty-handed" gift. When opened, that gift probably prompted an "Oh, how nice" reaction and eventually was relegated to some closet's top shelf. There's one factor that essentially separates these two gifts: it's the level of insight you have into the person based on the substance of the relationship. The better your understanding, the better the outcome and the more likely the recipient is to think of you whenever he or she uses your gift.

"That same dynamic exists between us and our customers. The more insightful and understanding we are of them, the more we can deliver exactly what they want. That's why we launched a campaign recently that, for the very first time, asked our company's consumers what's important to them."

STAYING CONFIDENT DURING ROUGH CONVERSATIONS

Nowhere is the Conviction Principle more important than during uncomfortable and tense conversations, the kind we all try hard to avoid.

One of my first memories of a conversation like that also goes back to fifth grade. I went to a wonderful school in New York City called the Riverdale Country School. In 1971, though, diversity among the student body wasn't what it is today. Out of thirty-six male students, no more than five or six were boys of color, which meant that they were always outnumbered.

Shortly after the Beatles broke up, a debate developed between Russell Jackson, an African American friend of mine, and several of my white classmates. The point of contention: who was better, the Beatles or the Jackson 5? Russell was a fan of the then-young Michael Jackson and his family. As the stalemate raged on, with both sides talking past each other, the notion that both sides should come away with their pride and dignity intact suddenly came to me.

Russell turned to me and asked, "Billy, what do you think?" I

replied, "Well, I think both will be famous for a long time. As performers and entertainers, I think the Jackson 5 are better. I think as
musician/songwriters, I would give the Beatles the edge."

At first I thought that reply would leave both sides feeling terribly unsatisfied, but I was amazed at what happened next. Because
everybody came away with a partial win, the air of conflict dissi-
pated, and the conversation calmly shifted to a topic of comfort for
all eleven-year-old boys: how yucky girls were.

Now, as a communications coach, I find myself in other types
of tense situations. Often I must find a way to coach unwilling clients. Sometimes people come to one of my media trainings firmly
convinced that they have all the skills they need and that the session will be a paint-by-numbers instruction that insults their intelligence and wastes their time. You might think a crabby and resistant
trainee would be a real anxiety provoker, but I've come to love the
challenge. There's nothing more gratifying than having hostile
skeptics awash in attitude leave four hours later proclaiming that
the training was one of the most beneficial things they've done in
a long time.

When you find yourself amid conversational tension, try these
tactics:

Validate; Don't Bully

Validating others' opinions, even if they're contrary to our own,
is mistakenly thought of as a sign of weakness in this era of cable-
news bombast. Civility has all but left modern discourse, as we have
been conditioned to think that bullying others into admitting we're
right and they're wrong is the ultimate sign of persuasiveness.

Find a Way to Agree

Highlighting even the tiniest sliver of common ground is such an outdated notion that it actually is fresh and new again. In addition to that, it is the ultimate sign of security and confidence to acknowledge another's opinion and find value in it, instead of belittling and steamrolling.

Point Out a Strength

Acknowledging people's strengths while telling them they've got some issue to resolve is a good way to bring balance to the conversation and avoid making them feel ashamed or embarrassed. Think of adopting the "critique sandwich" model. In it the critical meat of what you have to say is sandwiched between two acknowledgments of their strengths or something they do well.

THE HAND OF CONVICTION

Few things create an underwhelming first impression quite like a limp handshake. You know this, right? It's been drilled into your head ever since high school. Still, I feel I must mention it, because it's still all too common. Lucy Cherkasets, who coaches job seekers for Clarity Media Group, once worked in HR and has encountered more than her share of job seekers greeting her with the least confident of handshakes.

One in particular held out a hand so gently that it reminded Lucy of the way royalty extends a hand for someone to kiss.

Perhaps the most bizarre request I've ever gotten was the one about the "clamshake." A sales executive with a major corporation came to us primarily to hone his pitch to prospective clients, but his bosses added one more goal for the coaching session.

"We were wondering if you could talk to him about his hand-shake," the woman from the human resources department of his company said.

"His handshake? What's wrong with it?" I couldn't imagine it was one of those limp, dead-fish handshakes. I'd never met a sales person suffering from one of those.

"I know this sounds odd, but he has the sweatiest, clammiest handshake you've ever felt."

"Oh, wow," I said. "For a sales guy, that can be a deal breaker, I imagine," trying hard to validate the severity they were attach-ing to this problem. Part of our firm's success is never saying no, finding ways to help solve a problem even if it lies outside our core capabilities, so I said, "I'll certainly mention it if I feel there's an organic opening in the conversation to allude to it, but it might be too awkward. But I'll see what I can do."

When the day arrived for this trainee's session, the anticipation of having to shake hands with this guy was something right out of a Seinfeld episode. I had my handkerchief at the ready in my pocket. I warned my assistants, who typically are the ones to first welcome guests, about the likelihood of a damp greeting, and I was prepared with advice to help him go from moist to arid.

The first solution, the most radical, would be Botox injections in the hand. I know it sounds ridiculous, but doctors say that if you render the sweat glands inert, your palm will stay dry.

The second option would be to advise the salesman to keep a handkerchief in his pocket and, just before shaking a hand, to grab the hanky and blot the extra moisture.

The third possibility would be to have him say he's just getting over a cold and doesn't want to make the other person sick.

And if all else failed, the rep could claim to be a follower of the Howard Hughes and Donald Trump school of handshaking: just plain refusing to do it. But then, of course, he'd run the risk of seeming psychotically eccentric without the billions to justify it.

So in he walked. I took a deep breath and braced for some moisture. He extended his hand, and with an eagerness intended to belie
my dread, I heartily extended mine. They met. Wouldn't you know
it, his palm was as dry as mine. I was both shocked and relieved.

Although I was prepared with advice and solutions that day, I
never shared them with him. That would have been too bizarre.
But if you tend to get strange looks of apprehension from people
when you extend your hand, try some of the strategies I just mentioned. In those critically important opening seconds of any face-
to-face encounter, you don't want an unpleasant experience to be
what's remembered.

HOW TO STAND WITH CONVICTION

More important than your handshake is how you stand. Our posture affects more than the way others perceive us. According to
research from Harvard Business School, our posture affects our
feelings of confidence, which in turn affects our behavior. Study
participants who spent two minutes in "power postures" experienced a 20 percent increase in testosterone. Many people think of
testosterone as a male sex hormone, yet it's actually present in both
genders. When its level in the blood rises, it gives men and women
a boost in confidence.

But it's not just what you gain, it's also what you lose. Not only
did study participants experience a boost in testosterone, there was
also a 25 percent drop in the stress hormone cortisol. Blocking the
release of cortisol can help bring your anxiety level down.

In contrast, when study participants sat or stood in weaker positions, the opposite happened: cortisol levels surged 15 percent, and
subjects felt less confident and more stressed.

To stand with confidence, do what your mother always told
you: stand up straight. Use this head-to-toe guide.

Shoulders

DO

Pull them back to open the chest.

DON'T

Shrug them toward your ears.

Arms

DO

Create a ninety-degree angle between your forearms and upper arms. Keep them out in front of you, with your arms and hands soft and relaxed. This allows you to easily gesture if needed. There's never a long distance for them to travel, so your gestures don't become distracting.

Create a 90-degree angle between your forearms and upper arms.

When you are not using your hands, bring them together at the level of your belt buckle.

Allow your fingers to lightly touch.

DON'T

Use any of the Five Positions of Doubt (see page 120).

Hands

DO

Gesture to make a point, but don't keep your hands in constant motion or make the same gesture repeatedly. Also, it's best to keep them within the frame of your body instead of flailing them to the sides, where they can be distracting. When you are not using your hands, bring them together right around where your belt buckle would be. Allow your fingers to lightly touch, almost as if the fingers of your right hand are gently touching a ring on your left ring finger. Your palms should be facing in toward you with the backs of your hands facing your audience.

DON'T

Place your hands anywhere that makes your listeners think, "What is that person doing with her hands?" You don't want your listeners to be watching your hands. You want them to listen to what you have to say. In particular, stay away from the following:

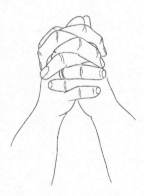

The Death Grip.
Tightly clasped hands create a look of tension and make you appear anxious.

The Finger Triangle.
Back in the 1980s, many TV reporters used the triangle, touching all their fingers together as they made a point. Any posture that was outdated even back in the 1990s is to be avoided at all costs.

The Fig-Leaf Position.
You did remember to get dressed this morning, right?

The Public Bathroom Pose.
In this posture, you rub your hands together repeatedly as if you were using an electric hand dryer.

Feet

DO
Shift your weight forward slightly onto the balls of your feet so you can feel a slight pressure in your toes. This will keep your weight forward so you are learning toward your audience.

DON'T
Get back on your heels. This position is not only more passive, it also makes it all too easy for you to get fidgety feet. When you're

speaking in a high-stakes situation, your body produces adrenaline, and while this provides a good energy spike, there's a definite
downside. Our bodies like to expel excess nervous energy, and the
most common portal through which it escapes is our feet. If you
watch people when they are nervous, you'll see this clearly. Some
sway from side to side. Others look almost as if they are marching
in place. These tics make you look fidgety and nervous, compro-
mising your projection of confidence to others. Standing with your
weight slightly forward makes it almost physically impossible for
you to become a moving target. Also avoid crossing your legs at
the shin. Over the years, I have discovered that when people are
nervous, they often lapse into this stance. It must be the standing
equivalent of the fetal position in terms of the security and comfort
it gives people, but it is far too easy to lose your balance in this pose
and stagger or even stumble. Falling down during a key speech or
presentation would not be good.

FIVE POSITIONS OF DOUBT

Have you ever watched what speakers do with their hands? If so,
you probably weren't paying much attention to what they were
saying. That's just the point. To boost your audience's focus on what
you're saying and increase your look of conviction, confidence, and
command, avoid these five hand and arm positions.

Behind Your Back

Though the pose works for speed skaters, it's too passive and apologetic for public speakers. It sends a visual signal that you are undeserving of people's attention.

Crossed over Your Chest

Also known as the Nikita Khrushchev pose, this comes across as defiant and judgmental, closes you off from your audience, and makes you seem less accessible. We also associate it from our childhood with the stance taken by a teacher or a parent before doling out punishment.

In Your Pockets

Nuns in Catholic schools condemn this pose for boys for the obvious reason. There are two other reasons to avoid it. A client of mine struck this pose with loose change in his pockets, and the jittery movement of his hands (another energy-expelling portal) made it sound like the neighborhood ice cream truck was approaching. I've also witnessed numerous speakers reach for their pockets after they're done gesticulating, only to fumble around for the opening. As my kids say, "Awkward."

On Your Hips

It's best to leave this pose to superheroes sporting tights and capes. Some people think that this position makes them appear authoritative and confident, but it's usually perceived as arrogant.

At Your Sides

We all look uncomfortable with our arms just dangling by our sides. The weight of the arms gives a little droop to the shoulders. It presents a problem for gesticulating, too. When your arms are at your sides, your hands have a greater distance to travel upward if you want to use them to stress a point. They also have a long way to fall to get back down into a resting position. In this position, gesticulating comes across more as a choreographed move than an organic motion.

I would be remiss to leave this section without a nagging reminder to never touch your face, stroke your beard, play with your hair, swoosh your hair off your face with a backward jerk of your head, or any other action that is perceived by your audience as an attempt at personal grooming.

HOW TO SIT WITH CONVICTION

Standing to speak commands more attention than sitting, but there are two scenarios in which standing seems inappropriate.

1. Fewer than eight people are sitting around a conference table.
2. You are speaking to an audience of work colleagues that is smaller than a standing-room-only crowd.

Achieving the right sitting position is just as important as your standing one. Slouch in your chair, and it will be an uphill battle selling your ideas. You'll not only look like you blend into the furniture, but you'll feel like it too. On the other end of the spectrum is what I call the electric-chair pose. When your feet are flat on the floor, your back is completely against the back of the chair, and your arms become one with the armrests, it looks as though your time is up.

You want to find the middle ground between those extremes. Try to acclimate yourself to this sitting position so you can grow to feel comfortable in it—because you must feel a sense of comfort to perform well.

Rest the middle of your forearms against the edge of the table.

Sit straight from the base of your spine.

Sit near the edge of the chair so your feet can touch the ground.

Adjust your chair so the table's edge meets your belt buckle.

Don't Look Up to Others

Before you sit down, make sure your chair (if it's adjustable) is set to its maximum height. You don't want to feel like George Bailey looking up at Mr. Potter from across the desk in *It's a Wonderful*

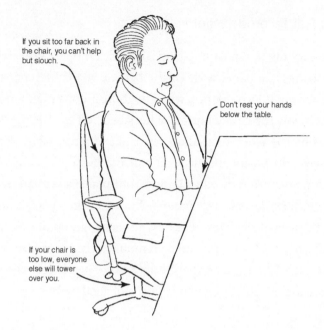

If you sit too far back in the chair, you can't help but slouch.

Don't rest your hands below the table.

If your chair is too low, everyone else will tower over you.

Life. One of the reasons TV news anchors look authoritative is because the anchor desk usually only comes up to just above the belt buckle. You never see it reaching the midchest area.

Note: if your chair rocks or swivels, resist the urge. The movement will make you look fidgety.

Belly Up to the Bar

Sheryl Sandberg has taught us how important it is to "lean in." I agree, but it's also true in the literal sense. If your shoulder blades are resting against the back of the chair, you're sitting back too far. At most, only the lowest part of your back should touch the vertical cushion. Your stomach should come right up to the edge of the table, but if your shoulders are over the table, you're slouching. Sit up straight from the base of your spine. You should feel a little pinch in the small of your back so you can sit both forward and straight up.

Wear a Full Tailored Jacket

If you are sitting down, your jacket is better left open, especially if you're sitting on a panel without the benefit of a conference table in front of you. It looks sloppy when the bottom of a man's necktie pops out below the closed button of his jacket. Of course, that's not nearly as bad as when men allow the sight of a bare shin to peek out between the bottom of a trouser cuff and the top of a sock—but then, I don't have to remind you how unthinkable it is to allow that to happen, now do I? Good. I didn't think so. After you sit down, grab both sides of the back vent of your jacket and pull it taut underneath your butt, the trick made famous in the 1980s film *Broadcast News*. It will eliminate that bumpy ridge just below the back collar of your jacket, giving you a more polished look.

Don't Get Too Comfy

If you are sitting in a chair that looks as though it could be in someone's living room instead of an office, don't get swallowed up by it. Sit near the edge to make sure your feet still touch the floor and you stay in a position that promotes mental alertness. Sitting back and getting comfy could promote a nap instead.

Get Your Elbows *on* the Table

We wouldn't want to incur the wrath of the Emily Post Institute (one of our clients), but if you are at a conference table or even a business lunch, keep your hands above the table. Having your hands in your lap, below the table, is polite in a personal setting, but too passive in a business one. The middle of your forearms should be resting against the edge of the table. From that position, it's also easier to gesture while you speak.

Get a Leg Up

More than 75 percent of my female clients ask me, "What should I do with my legs?" If you have short legs, it can feel unsettling to not have your feet touch the floor. And if you followed my earlier advice and raised your chair to its highest level, this problem can be exacerbated. It will also compromise your gravitas quotient if you're exposed head to toe without a conference table obscuring the sight of your feet dangling in midair. Try this: cross them at the ankle and tuck them underneath the chair, perhaps even resting on the swivel base of the chair rather than the floor. Of course, the more you sit forward in the seat, the better off you'll be. Even if you have longer legs, I bet you'll find that this pose allows you to sit up even taller in the chair, which is always good for executive presence.

HOW TO DRESS WITH CONVICTION

You won't believe the downright awkward urgings clients have asked me to deliver to the people they've sent for training. Even the guy who left the bottle of Scope mouthwash on the desk of the colleague with bad breath in that ad campaign of yesteryear was afforded the luxury of anonymity. No such luck for me. My cringe-worthy advice is always delivered face-to-face.

So even though the following list of fashion do's and don'ts might sound like common sense, know that it's not common sense for everyone. If you read this list and think *I know all this*, congratulate yourself on your knowledge and simply read the following section to see how you would use the Conviction Principle to deliver this kind of dicey information to someone else.

If, however, you read this list and recognize a faux pas, take corrective action.

The Bushy Brow

A successful CEO in the retail clothing business was about to go on TV with eyebrows that looked as if they had been given extensions made of Brillo. His executive assistant pulled me aside and pleaded with me to find some way to tell him they needed to be trimmed. I was tempted to ask her if they had some hedge clippers so I could do it myself. So again, I tried to make it seem as though the advice I was offering was done for strictly strategic purposes and completely tied to the goal he was trying to accomplish. Here's what I told him:

"The most important factor in allowing TV viewers to feel a sense of connection with you is for there to be eye contact. You want them to have full view of your eyes—that's essential in building trust and likability. Anything obstructing that has to be corrected. So sometimes women will be on camera, and if they're wearing their hair down and against their face, they'll actually obscure the viewers' ability to see one of their eyes. For you, your eyebrows could create that same disconnection. If you trim them, you'll be allowing viewers to fully connect with your warmth and engagement."

Success or Bust

One female cookbook author needed to be told to minimize her cleavage. Of course, I didn't convey that thought to her in those exact words. Instead I told her that a smart strategic wardrobe choice for network morning shows might be something a little less provocative and sexy. I shared with her the well-documented theory as to why Deborah Norville was removed as Jane Pauley's replacement on *Today* in 1991, after only fifteen months on the job. The conventional thinking back then was that female viewers preferred not to invite into the living room a woman whom they feared their husbands would want to invite into the bedroom—or at least that's what male network executives thought. So the message to this author followed that reasoning:

"Predominantly these shows are watched by women, and cookbooks are overwhelmingly purchased by women. Yes, we want the value of what you've written to come across, but we also want them to like you. If they like you, they'll be more inclined to click the ADD TO CART button on Amazon. If they feel threatened by you, they probably will not. So with your wardrobe, if you have the choice between alluring or slightly conservative, I would edge toward the conservative side. Why risk it?"

Again, my advice was not based on my being judgmental or indicating that I thought she looked a little trampy. It was to tell her how her clothing choices can help her achieve what she wants, by laying out a rational argument for why certain choices work better than others. That was actually the second time I had to give that wardrobe guidance. The first time was to a woman in the education field who rather immodestly responded, "I'm sorry, but I can't really help it. I'm just plain sexy!" For her, we skipped the confidence-building part of the session.

Practice Fastidious Oral Hygiene

After she was interviewed on TV, a print journalist sent me the clip and asked me for help on ways to seem less fidgety in a TV studio. After watching it, though, I realized what she needed more was advice on her dingy teeth. Because she is a beautiful woman, that one negative feature stands out all the more. So here's what I told her:

"You look great on camera . . . but keep in mind, you're being interviewed by a professional TV host sitting across from you. All of those anchors get their teeth professionally whitened. When the camera cuts back and forth providing that immediate juxtaposition, our teeth can look a little dingy by comparison, even though they look perfectly fine in person. Just something to keep in mind."

Here, the comfort level of the advice hinges on her being in the distorted reality of a TV studio, where what looks fine elsewhere can fall short because the bar has been raised artificially.

PITCH-PERFECT POINTER

If you are a guy who attends many evening events—business dinners, shows, and panels, often extending into the night—keep an electric razor in your briefcase, shoulder bag, or suitcase. Five o'clock shadow makes you look tired, not fresh and crisp. While you're at it, also stash two pairs of collar stays and a pair of inexpensive cuff links (they sell cloth ones at Brooks Brothers), so you're always looking crisp and well put together. I worked with Charlie Rose in the 1980s at CBS, and for Christmas the staff wanted to get him a lifetime supply of collar stays. In the mornings right before we taped the show, his collars would be about as straight as a snowboarding half pipe. We kept stopping him in the hallway, saying, "You can't go on the air like that."

STRENGTHEN YOUR CONVICTION MUSCLE

There are two reasons why so many of us settle for threadbare clichés, slouching, and limp handshakes: habit and complacency.

Let's face it, relentless self-improvement is not for sissies. It can be hard work. It often means breaking habits we've clung to for most of our adult lives. And you know what they say? Behavior is one of the hardest things to change.

Your chances of improvement are far greater if you're the type of person who listens to trusted advice, takes it seriously, and recognizes that sometimes other people know what's best. At the other end of the spectrum are those who nod their heads, pretend to hear, and forget advice almost as soon as they've heard it.

Very rarely do I deal with the latter, except the time I media-trained the reality star and former supermodel Janice Dickinson. I was prepping Janice for a media tour to publicize her memoir called *No Lifeguard on Duty*. In the session, I asked her the question every book author needs to hit out of the park if they intend to sell any books: "What's your book about?" It's such a simple question, but you'd be surprised how many authors stammer and stumble through a thoroughly forgettable answer.

Janice's original answer was: "It's a cautionary tale of sex, drugs, and rock 'n' roll, fashion, fashion, fashion, and 'thrival.'" My desire to steer her away from the cliché "sex, drugs, and rock 'n' roll" was surpassed only by my curiosity as to what the hell "thrival" meant.

"It's a word I've coined that's a cross between thriving and survival." The room went momentarily silent as we all pondered this new contribution to the English language. Her sycophantic personal assistant was the first to speak up: "Oh, I *love* that word!"

His obligatory fawning made it more difficult for me to tell the empress that she had no clothes on.

"The dictionary is chock-full of established options. Let's get our money's worth out of them." This was my way of conveying one of my fundamental rules of the road: If a word you're using to communicate gets rejected in Words with Friends, you shouldn't use it.

"And besides," I told her, "we want you to sound fresh and original, and 'sex, drugs, and rock 'n' roll' is overused."

"OK, so what would you recommend?" she asked.

"Well, how about . . . 'It's a full-access glimpse of a time when actors, rock stars, athletes, and supermodels played together with an intensity rarely seen before and redefined the whole notion of celebrity. This book takes you behind not just the velvet ropes, but behind the closed doors of VIP playgrounds.'"

"Oh I *love* that! Write that down . . . write that down!" she implored her notebook-toting assistant. Janice was, as you would expect, a total hoot. How could the woman who claims to have created the word *supermodel* be anything less? At the end of three hours, she professed her deep appreciation for my help, air-kissed me on each cheek, and signed my book, dotting the *i* in Janice with a big heart.

A few days later, I was hunkered down in my den, waiting for my eccentric and flamboyant pupil to be interviewed by Elizabeth Vargas on *Good Morning America*. Very early in the interview, the basic question was asked: "So Janice, what's your book about?"

Quickly my giddy anticipation morphed into shock and dismay as Janice circled all the way back to her original answer, the one I thought we had agreed was far too clichéd and meaningless to drive book sales: "It's a cautionary tale of sex, drugs, and rock 'n' roll, fashion, fashion, fashion, and 'thrival.'" What? What happened to our new and improved answer? Had her flunky not written it down? It was as if that whole section of the training had been expunged from her memory.

It went from bad to worse when Elizabeth Vargas, in her most incredulous, what-the-hell-are-you-talking-about-girl tone of voice scrunched up her face and asked, "Thrival?" You didn't have to possess ESP to predict that.

But thankfully, there are the sublime cases to balance the ridiculous. Around the same time, I had the sheer joy of coaching Trisha Meili, the courageous woman who is better known as the Central Park jogger. Meili was an investment banker who had gone jogging in the park early one evening at dusk and was viciously attacked by a gang of violent thugs, or so the police originally assumed.

She was savagely beaten to within an inch of her life in what may have been the first reported case of "wilding." It's believed that one of the suspects during a police interrogation may have referred to the attack as doing "the wild thing" and it was the misinterpretation that created the new term.

Years after the attack, Trisha decided to come forward and finally reveal her identity to the world. I had the honor of helping her prepare for what was shaping up to be a long sit-down interview with Katie Couric, probably two hours long. Trisha was a lovely, warm, intelligent woman who exuded a sense of grace. Meeting and working with her had a profound effect on me. Perhaps I had expected to encounter someone who, despite her miraculous recovery, harbored a deep bitterness for her profound and random misfortune. To my amazement, she exhibited not one ounce of negativity.

We prepped for a wide variety of questions we expected Katie to ask, including:

- What was your life like before the attack?
- What do you remember about that night?
- Did you have any hesitation to run in the park that late?
- What are your feelings toward your attackers?
- What was the most difficult part of your recovery? (We media people love to ask that slightly sanitized version of "When did you hit rock bottom?" because it usually gets the interview to take an emotional turn.)

But then I presented her with one she hadn't been expecting: "When did you realize that your story had become national news, even world news, and that millions of people were following your ordeal?"

Trisha gave me a fairly vague, abstract, and theoretical answer. The fact that I can't recall it here is testament to how forgettable it was. She could tell by the look on my face that I wasn't loving her reply.

"OK, I admit it. Not great. What do you think my answer should be?"

"I'd simply refer to something you described in your book—when you saw those dozen long-stemmed roses from Frank Sinatra in your hospital room."

"Really? You think I should say that?" Trisha asked.

"Trust me. I've never been more certain of anything, ever."

And wouldn't you know, several minutes into the interview, Katie asked the same question: "When did you first become aware that the entire country was following your story and praying for your recovery?"

A schoolgirl grin came over Trisha's face before she delivered the line with authenticity—not at all canned or contrived. Katie's face suddenly flashed that trademark megawatt smile for which she is handsomely compensated, and she and Trisha then had an adorably giggly and girly moment, like teens at a slumber party discussing the new cute boy in school. It was a total "moment" in the show and one I was proud to have had a hand in creating.

The point I'm trying to make is not that I always know best. It's that without a game plan and practice, it will be hard to raise your game in the conviction department.

What Trisha and Janice make abundantly clear is that we all have it within our control to say something memorable. Yes, the content has to be good, but equally important is delivering it with conviction. I hope this chapter has given you a number of different thought-provoking ways to adjust your swing. Now it's up to you to go out and lock them into your new muscle memory.

8

THE CURIOSITY PRINCIPLE

*Wisdom is the reward you get for a lifetime of listening
when you'd have preferred to talk.*

—Doug Larson

HAVE YOU EVER come home from a party and felt exhausted, as if every conversation sucked the life from you like one of those Dementor creatures in Harry Potter? With any luck, those occasions are more than balanced by the social events that leave you feeling invigorated and happy.

What makes the difference? The food? The music? The setting? Perhaps. My guess is that the biggest determinant of whether the evening was a crashing bore or a roaring good time was the caliber of the conversation. And the key ingredient that makes a conversation truly great is curiosity. Too bad it's an ingredient that's becoming harder and harder to find.

My wife, a journalism professor, and I often share our observations on everyone's conversational skills whenever we get home from social functions. (What can I say? It's an occupational hazard for us both.) Over the years, we've concluded that some conversations are laborious and clumsy, whereas others seem effortless and elegant.

Great conversationalists are seldom the raconteurs holding court in front of a group of adoring fans. Instead, they're the ones who are as interested as they are interesting. They pay attention to what you have to say and are intrigued to want to know more. And they wear this engagement not on their sleeves but on their faces, signaling through their expressiveness their delight in the give-and-take of such social interactions.

THE BENEFITS OF CURIOSITY

The majority of us have no idea what kind of vibe we give off when we're listening. We may very well be captivated, yet we inadvertently come off as if we're really thinking about something else.

I witness this contradiction just about every time I speak to an audience. My eye will unfortunately catch someone in the audience whose facial expression resembles that of Jack Nicholson in the final scene from *One Flew over the Cuckoo's Nest*: mouth slightly open, head cocked to one side, eyes staring straight ahead at nothing in particular. More times than not, though, it's that guy—the one with the vacant stare—who comes up to me afterward to say, "You know I really loved what you had to say, especially your point about . . ." and then go on to discuss the speech in great detail.

This is not to say that everyone who gives you a detached, blank stare is digging what you're saying. What you can assume, however, is this: there are times when *you* accidentally communicate "I'm checked out" when you really want to communicate "I'm hanging on your every word."

No one can crawl inside your brain and see that you are really listening and hearing. You have to show it. So as counterintuitive as it may seem, in conversation, it can be just as important to be Pitch Perfect in the way you listen as the way you speak.

The Curiosity Principle will help you to overcome this mismatch between how you feel inside and how you appear on the outside. It will also help you to:

Fuel Important Conversations

When you're suddenly alone with your boss or with a key potential client at a business gathering, the last thing you want is for the conversation to lapse into some meaningless exchanges and then an awkward silence. People respond better when you look and act mentally involved and intrigued.

Score Personal Points

Giving someone your undivided attention is the new pinnacle of customer service. So many of the other methods of flattery we resort to (like heavy-handed compliments) can make us seem like shameless suck-ups. Curiosity and genuine interest is much more subtle. Customers and clients want to be heard, and they feel flattered by undistracted attention.

Take Someone's Pulse

The more often you listen with curiosity, the more skilled you will be at reading people, an enormously valuable asset to develop and fine-tune. Then once you gain a clear understanding of what makes people tick, you'll be able to more easily incorporate the Draper Principle (chapter 9) and steer the conversation in a direction that's enjoyable for them. Many people never strengthen the muscle required to read others because, rather than listening, they're too busy waiting for their turn to talk. That's why social workers, reporters, police detectives, psychologists, rabbis, and priests are often good at reading people. Their jobs require them to be constantly listening and observing.

Displaying a sense of curiosity and interest is one more way to stand out from your competitors, as people who demonstrate this ability are increasingly rare.

THE ELEMENTS OF CURIOSITY

The art of conversation seems to be going the way of the pay phone. Hardly anybody uses it, so you don't find much of it around. That's because many people mistakenly believe that the most important skill a conversationalist needs is the ability to talk endlessly. So they talk *at* people rather than *with* them.

In reality, the best conversationalists are extremely good listeners, and they display three rare characteristics:

Interest

Being a good conversationalist requires attentiveness and enthusiasm. It doesn't mean that you have to create a new BFF. The trick is to listen for some nugget of information that inspires you to want to know more about a particular topic. For instance, if a client mentions that her husband just bought her a kayak for her birthday, that's an opportunity to seize. It's only natural to ask any of the following questions to gain greater insight:

- Are you an experienced kayaker or just learning it? (The answer would tell me whether she's outdoorsy or a sports enthusiast.)
- Is there a place to use it near where you live? (Now I'll know what community she lives in—and a way to take the conversation in a new direction.)
- Was this a surprise or had you asked for one? (This might give me some insight into what kind of relationship she has with her spouse.)
- Is this something you'll just do on weekends or might you indulge midweek? (Her answer might tell me to what degree she's married to her job.)
- Anybody else in the family already looking to get their hands on it? (Now I've opened the door to finding out if she has children—another topic on which we may find common ground.)

This approach provides you with a much more organic and less forced way to learn more about someone than the clumsier, straightforward questions we often ask: So what are your hobbies? Where do you live? What do you do for a living? What does your husband do? Do you have kids? Those sound like an interrogation, an unpleasant scenario for anyone.

Generosity

Your likability is central to your success; people will seek you out if you are a generous conversationalist. If you're a selfish hog who talks only about yourself, you'll quickly become known as the crashing bore everyone wants to avoid. But if you include people, ask for their input, seek out their stories, thoughtfully consider their dissenting opinions without bombastic ridicule, you will exude an aura others gravitate to.

Modesty

It's easy to trick ourselves into thinking that modesty and humility have no place in today's übercompetitive business world, where we're all told to advertise ourselves as diligently as Disney markets the magic of its theme parks. But in the art of self-promotion, there's no need to be shameless. It just requires a little finesse. If you come barreling up to a few strangers at a networking event and blindside them with your "elevator pitch," you're going to reek of desperation. I know it's hard when you're feeling a real sense of urgency to pull in new business, but a much more professional and confident approach would be to hold back and make people ask about you.

What happens if no one seems interested in popping the question? Try teasing them into asking. If they're blathering on about clients who don't pay their bills on time, say, "I also see a lot of that in my work," or "Fortunately, I don't have to contend with that too much in our business." Only somebody thick as a brick would not be lured into asking, "Oh yeah, what do you do?"

There's also a strategic advantage to going second. It allows you to identify which area of your business might be of greatest interest to the other person. If I'm sitting next to someone on a flight and he mentions that he works for a luxury fashion designer, it gives me two options. I can put forth the teaser by saying, "Oh that's interesting. We just did a job earlier this month for Armani," which invariably prompts the "Oh, really? What line of work are you in?" Or I can sit back a bit and wait for the question, at which point I'll say we're a communications-coaching firm that works across a number of industries, including luxury retail. Usually that gets the conversation cooking.

Self-promotion and modesty are not mutually exclusive.

THE FRIENDLY FILIBUSTER

The title of this section is almost as much an oxymoron as "friendly fire." What does this arcane legislative procedure have to do with conversational skills? Well, I'm sure at some point we have all found ourselves ensnared in a conversation with someone impersonating Jimmy Stewart's character in *Mr. Smith Goes to Washington*, minus the altruistic charm. Those relentless gabbers talk endlessly about themselves and seem oblivious to the fact that there are other people who might actually want to say something. They rarely, if ever, listen to others.

We all do this at least occasionally. Case in point: Harvard researchers tell us that many of us spend more than 40 percent of our time talking about ourselves. Here, however, I'm referring to a special breed of conversational hog that I call the Egg-Timer Narcissist (ETN for short). In less time than it takes to soft-boil an egg, these self-centered bores plot and execute a master plan that flips the conversation from whatever you might be saying back to their favorite topic: them.

It doesn't matter how serious your topic is. You could be talking about how an intruder broke into your house while you were home. Then, in the middle of a sentence, before you get to the reveal of whether everything turned out okay, an ETN will interrupt with total banality:

"Oh I know. We were pricing home-security systems last month, because we saw this ad on TV last week for burglar alarms—you know, the kind you can control from your smartphone. Isn't that stuff just amazing? By the way, speaking of TV ads, did you know our oldest son is selling ad time for the local NBC station? He just got hired last month and already he's one of the top performers among his peers. In fact he's been such a standout that the other day his boss took him aside and . . ."

I wish I could say this is an exaggeration, but, if anything, it's an understated example.

By now you are so far off the topic that to bring it up again would make *you* look like the butt-in. We've all been in that position when it's not worth the energy it takes to engage in this conversational tug-of-war. The path of least resistance is to just listen to this rambling, inane nonsense, and quietly plan an escape strategy.

An old friend of ours was famous for this style of obliviousness. Every holiday, my wife and I would host him in our home. He invariably would plunk himself right in the middle of the chaotic kitchen at crunch time and drone on about what numskulls his bosses were. All the while I would be cooking on six burners and darting around the room like the Iron Chef. It's a miracle that I never once scalded him with boiling pasta water on the way from stove to sink. Come to think of it, maybe that's all it would have taken to regain some culinary peace and quiet.

Sometimes at a party, if I've had the misfortune of encountering two Egg-Timer Narcissists, I'll make a point to introduce them to each other. Then I'll step back and watch the games begin. I would imagine that it was much like watching a *Tyrannosaurus rex* and a *Giganotosaurus* square off in prehistoric times. Mutual annihilation of two aggressive creatures can sometimes make for fun spectating.

Egg-Timer Narcissists used to be a rare breed, but their ranks seem to be growing exponentially. Researchers at San Diego State University have found, for instance, that Millennials (also called Generation Y) show more traits of narcissism than members of Generation X (born between 1965 and 1980) or Boomers (born after WWII and before 1965). The psychologist Jean Twenge prefers the term *Generation Me* for Millennials. This apparent surge in narcissism might stem from the era we live in, the one that will be forever known for bestowing on all of us our own broadcast network. What with blogging, Facebook posting, tweeting, pinning, Instagramming, Snapchatting, and more, many of us are publishing the equivalent of daily newspapers about our own lives. The rise of all these amazing new ways to communicate has unquestionably caused one clear consequence: our verbal communication skills are suffering. There's a different dynamic to texting and status updates than there is to talking. Texting and tweeting is about "What am I going to say next?" It's a performance, much like delivering a monologue. You are less inclined to sit back and allow someone else to ruminate. Rather than converse with others, people digitally talk *at* one another.

Boomers and Gen X were born *before* this technology was invented. As a result, we learned how to converse the old-fashioned way: face to face and by a telephone that was connected to the wall by a cord. The younger you are, the more likely it is that some of your initial conversations took place with your fingertips rather than your mouth.

But no matter what your age, the scourge of narcissism presents you with a wonderful opportunity to stand out. In a business setting where everyone is talking, it's the person who listens with curiosity who becomes the most noticeable.

ANATOMY OF A CONVERSATION

Because you are reading this, I doubt you are prone to filibustering your friends. But chances are there are at least some times when your spirit is willing but your mouth is just too much.

I've met perfectly well-meaning friends for lunch and listened as they conversationally busted out of the barn like wild horses galloping off never to return. I sat there thinking, "No. There's no way he can continue focusing only on himself the entire lunch." Once back at the office, I invariably find an e-mail of regret: "Gee, I'm so sorry. I just realized I never asked how you're doing." That's an example of succumbing to the temptation of not letting go of the floor once you have it, and it can arise for many reasons: excitement, nerves, the Red Bull you chugged just before lunch, you name it. To help you prevent this phenomenon, let's dissect the various parts of the conversation where you don't want to act like an ETN.

The Opening

The ETN opens the conversation by looking for ways to dominate. In a worst-case scenario, ETNs launch straight into a pitch or story without getting to know the other players in the conversation. The curious listener, on the other hand, opens with questions. Do your homework ahead of time. Learn as much as you can about someone before your first conversation. That way you can ease into the conversation by asking someone about his or her hobbies, family, or vacation plans.

The Middle

This is the meat of the conversation. ETNs make it all about them. If you secretly worry that you might fall into this dreaded category, keep track of how many times you prompt input from the other person during your next conversation. Once is not enough. Whether your entire exchange is two minutes long or two hours, it's meant to be a give-and-take. As a general rule, try to listen and ask questions for at least half of the conversation.

The Close

I realized the importance of closing when I bumped into an old classmate on Madison Avenue. We were both heading downtown toward Fifty-Seventh Street, so we walked and talked for a few blocks. The conversation was going fine, albeit mainly focused on him. I was in the middle of a sentence when he spotted someone else he knew walking by us in the opposite direction. "I'm going to walk with him for a while now," he abruptly blurted out. And astonishingly, he did an about-face and began walking uptown, no doubt to bend that poor sucker's ear for a few blocks. His clumsy close left me stunned. Of course the proper thing to do if he wanted to make a switch would have been to stop the other person and say, "Hey, Marcus, wow, good to see you! Marcus, this is Bill McGowan, a classmate from high school. Bill, Marcus and I went to college together. [*To Marcus*] You know, I've been meaning to reach out to you for a couple of weeks now, because there's something I wanted to ask you. Bill, I hope you don't mind if I grab this chance to catch up with Marcus. It was really great to see you."

Something along those lines would have helped reassure me that my friend had indeed not been raised by a pack of wolves.

Recalling that episode made me think of how clumsily many people end conversations at work parties or conventions. Consider the following exit strategies often used during networking events and cocktail parties:

"**Will you excuse me?**" This is just plain rude. The literal translation for that is, "I can't bear to be trapped in the conversation with you one more minute, and you're not important enough for me to find a more graceful way out of it."

"**I'm going to refill my drink.**" It amazes me how frequently people lean on this tired cliché. Keep in mind how badly the conversational mate you've just ditched will feel if he or she glances over and sees you in a different conversation cluster, instead of where you are supposed to be—at the bar.

"**I'm sure you've talked to me longer than you probably wanted to.**" This drips of apology, and downgrades your stature. Why plant any idea in the other person's head that you're not worthy of their time.

True ETNs often don't close at all. They sometimes just walk away without a good-bye. Or they go on so long about themselves that *you* end up walking away without a good-bye.

Politicians have it so easy. They have staffers (the ones usually carrying the bottle of hand sanitizer) who walk up to them during the moment a conversation starts to lag, die, or go sideways and say, "Senator, we're running late for our next appointment."

For those of us who are not elected officials, we must learn to do it on our own. End the conversation sooner rather than later. You want to leave people wanting more. You don't want to leave them thinking, *Thank goodness that's over with.* Start your exit once big chunks of dead air creep in or you begin to cover ground already covered.

In much the same way that diet experts and nutritionists recommend you eat something before going to a party where there's going to be a lot of food, I say you should bulk up on something else: believable, original excuses for exiting a painfully awkward or one-sided conversation. The law of averages says you'll need to pull at least one or two out of your back pocket. Here are a handful of suggestions:

> **The Weekend Excuse:** "Oh, I promised our babysitter I'd check in with her before (give the current time)—will you excuse me a sec?"

> **The Weekday Excuse:** "My daughter has a big test tomorrow, and I just want to call her and see how the studying is coming along. It's been really great speaking with you."

> **The Anytime Excuse, Version 1:** "I brought a dish that needs to be heated up, so I'm going to hit the kitchen to take care of that. Maybe we can resume our chat a little later."

> **The Anytime Excuse, Version 2:** "By the way, do you know what time the party is over? [*Listen for the answer.*] Oh, I better call and reserve a car. Will you excuse me while I make that call?"

Now if you happen to be conversing with an ETN, ignore everything I just said. Extricating yourself from them does not need to be as subtle as you might think. You're dealing with some pretty dense people here, so what might seem sledgehammer obvious to you may barely register with an ETN. A line like, "I'm only staying a short while and there are a few other people I want to touch base with, so I hope you'll excuse me" should work just fine.

REVVING DOWN A MOTORMOUTH

Which of the five sense organs is the most important for us to succeed in conversation? By now you probably realize that it's not your mouth but your ears. Without a keen ability to listen, we are at a loss for developing the most effective strategy for how to be persuasive with others.

Consider:

- It's only by listening that you'll gain important pieces of information about people that you can use to tailor your pitch. So instead of turning to your boss with something bland like, "How was your weekend?" you'll be able to trigger a more in-depth and substantive conversation by asking, "By the way, how's your daughter's semester abroad going?"
- When you interrupt or talk *over* someone who is angry or irritated, you only stoke the flames of their irritation. Listening, on the other hand, sends a signal that you're approaching the conflict with an open mind and flexibility instead of stubbornness. Once you understand someone's concerns, you can more effectively address them. If you've ever said to someone, "Go ahead and tell me how you see this situation," the other person often takes a deep breath to relax, slows down their speaking pace, and becomes less manic and argumentative.
- You can never fine-tune the skill of reading people if you're always in a hurry to talk about yourself.

As you listen, pay attention to your facial expression and avoid the bored-looking scowl that so commonly afflicts many listeners (see next section for specific advice). Also, express your enthusiasm for the story someone is telling, but stay away from empty platitudes. Filler like, "wow, awesome," "yeah I know," and "so interesting" signal that your mind is really elsewhere. To truly sound engaged, respond with specific statements that prove just how intently you've been listening. Even better, ask a follow-up question that prompts the other person to share a story.

Listening has saved my ass from getting completely engulfed in a number of thorny situations. One of them happened early in 2013. I was hired to train a group of actors and their showrunner (the creative driving force behind the show) just before the program's premiere. When a show first goes on the air, it usually generates media interest, and it can be helpful to have someone like me suggest certain interview answers that ignite viewer interest in the show. For some Hollywood types, having a session like this land on their calendar is embraced with all the enthusiasm of a required trip to the Department of Motor Vehicles. I don't blame them. If roles were reversed, I would see it too as an unpleasant, unproductive waste of valuable time. So not surprisingly, this group told their publicists that they had zero interest in showing up for their session with me. They said that the only reason they were coming was because the network was making them do it.

In walked the actors and the show's creator. They were charming and warm and gave no hint as to how little they wanted to be spending the afternoon with me. I tried to convince myself that the publicist had gotten it all wrong and that they were actually really psyched for the coaching session. Then after we dispensed with the pleasantries, the show's creator began expressing his deep disdain for the notion of what I was there to teach them: the art of a sound bite.

"I've created something here that is thoughtful and subtle and nuanced, and the notion of trying to summarize that in a pithy and catchy quote is distasteful to me," he said.

At that point, the whole conversation could have gone one of two ways. While he was expressing his disdain for the sound bite, I could have mentally rolled my eyes, thought about how difficult he was going to be to train, and generally allowed the sound waves coming from his mouth to travel right past me and right on out one of our open windows. That strategy probably would have resulted in a verbal tug of war, with me telling him why sound bites were important and him telling me where I could shove those sound bites.

Instead, I listened closely and asked a few questions. I figured it wasn't a stretch to assume that, by association, I was distasteful also, because I was the guy trying to get him to speak that way. Rather than have him see *me* as the adversary, I wanted him to see me as a partner, a teammate. So I tried to morph the "me-against-you" dynamic into one of "us against them."

"Listen," I said. "I get it. What you've put on the screen is complex and thoughtful stuff [which was true]. If we were playing by our rules, we wouldn't have to manufacture fifteen-second sound bites. But for better or worse, we're playing by the media's rules tomorrow, and this is the currency they trade in. So if we want the results we're after—for them to frame the show the way we want them to—then just for tomorrow let's communicate it in a language they understand."

Over the next four hours, we crafted a concise story that he and the other actors felt comfortable with and that media outlets would find appealing and prompt readers to say, "Hey, this show sounds interesting."

What determines success or failure in your dealings with people may come down to a basic judgment call on your part: Do I hold my tongue and not say what I really think, or do I pull the trigger and say what's really on my mind? Remember the executive whom I told needed important interpersonal social skills? That may have been right for that setting, but had I chosen that tactic years earlier during a pivotal networking lunch, my business might not have gotten off the ground.

It was 2003, and my business was just finding its way, looking to get some traction. Outside of media companies, we didn't have too many major-league gets on the client list. During those lean years, I probably would have agreed to have lunch with John Gotti at Sparks Steak House if I'd thought it would lead to new business. Then came a big break. As a result of something pretty damn close to a cold call, I managed to get a lunch with a well-connected guy in PR. The first thing I noticed was that he seemed as though he didn't want to be there, even though he'd agreed to meet. The conversation was strained. I asked him a question that he clearly thought I should've known the answer to because he practically barked his reply at me. He had a clipped, abrupt way of speaking, which I attributed to his growing annoyance with sitting across from me. It felt like a Match.com date gone bad.

After ten minutes or so of what I perceived to be hostility, I was close to saying, "Listen, we haven't even ordered our food, and it's clear you don't want to be here. Why don't I go out this door and you go out that one? No harm, no foul."

I took a deep breath as I listened to him finish his sentence. I suddenly realized there was something about the nature of our conversation that wasn't working for him. I thought, "Just keep this going. Stop taking it personally and feeling wounded. Get this thing on some proper footing and everything will be OK."

I tried to bring the conversation to a different place, to an article I'd recently read in *PR Week*. It seemed to be a topic he was interested in because suddenly he became more palatable and my lunch went down slightly less crooked. And then to my utter shock, outside the restaurant while saying good-bye, he said, "So I'd be happy to connect you with a few people who I think could be enormously helpful in growing your client base." Had he been testing me in some way? I had no idea. But within two months, he had landed for us a Fortune 100 global powerhouse of a company that was a leader in its industry. Soon, six or so other heavy-hitter clients sprouted off that first one. We were on our way, and all because my decision that day was restraint.

Why did I decide not to tell him off but did decide to say something to the other executive whom I called out for her bad interpersonal skills? It all comes down to reading people, a skill you can develop only if you are a good listener.

KEEP THE BLANK STARE FOR YOUR POKER GAME

As strange as it may sound, during just about every training session, I touch on how to achieve the proper listening facial expression. I've had coaching sessions with some high-profile clients during which we analyze just this technique alone. We sit and watch selected freeze frames from their TV interviews and discuss what the look on their face is communicating, which research indicates speaks much louder than the words they say.

Even those people who muster a certain level of enthusiasm while they're speaking will emotionally and expressively downshift when they become the listener. Their engagement seems to dissipate, or worse, the corners of their mouths turn down, they furrow their brow a bit and sometimes even squint their eyes: all completely natural things to do when we're concentrating hard on something. The problem is, to  an audience or your conversation partner, that facial expression is usually interpreted as, "I haven't the slightest idea what you're talking about." Lots of people fall victim to this. It's an expression that comedian Taylor Orci, of the YouTube channel Broken People, brilliantly termed BRF: bitchy resting face.

What you want to look like is
the complete opposite, something
I call BFF, or best-friend face. It's
the curious expression we have
on our faces when we are listening to our best friend tell us a
great story. The perfect BFF is a
quarter smile.

Not long ago, I was training a
cosmetic surgeon and author. She
was the head of plastic surgery for
a prominent California hospital, and she has the best and most consistent BFF I'd ever seen.

She came into the office one morning for media-interview training, and during the first ninety minutes, I couldn't help but marvel
at her natural ability to hold the most pleasant and agreeable facial
expression. She didn't even flinch at the nasty, snarky questions I
threw at her during practice interviews, like, "When did you stop
ripping off Medicare?" Normally in the face of a question that filthy,
the interviewee's instinct is to adopt a facial expression that reflects
either their utter contempt for the interviewer or sheer panic. But
she just sat there, looking like she was not the slightest bit intimi-
dated.

"I have to tell you, in all the years I've been doing this," I told her,
"I've never seen anyone with your natural ability to convey such a
sense of utter calm and confidence while being barraged with questions. I mean, I even asked you some things to test whether you'd
lose your patience and bare your fangs at me."

Her answer left me somewhat speechless. "Well, a little shot
of Botox here" (she pointed to the left corner of her mouth) "and a
little shot of Botox here" (she then pointed to the right corner of her
mouth) "and actually the corners of my mouth can't turn down."
Her response made me wish I had Botoxed my jaw, because I was
pretty sure mine had hit the floor after hearing that one.

The good news is that you don't need Botox to be able to smile. You just need a little awareness and some practice. Here's why it's so important for your business and career. A BFF can help you:

- **Appear honest.** Study participants rated people as more sincere and sociable if they were smiling than if their faces were neutral.
- **Earn more money.** Waitresses who served with a big smile reaped much bigger tips than those who served patrons with only a small smile.
- **Make others feel good.** Smiling has been shown to boost not only your own mood, but also the moods of others around you. It also helps you feel and appear more confident.
- **Be more likable.** In a study that examined thirty-seven facial expressions and how onlookers interpreted them, people with a friendly, happy facial expression were rated as more attractive than people with any other expression.
- **Look younger.** OK, now I've really got your attention. Forget the face-lift that makes you look like an attraction at Madame Tussauds wax museum. When you smile, you organically lift everything. Clients are often shocked at how much older they look when they let their facial expressions flatten out.

You don't need to walk around with a huge smile plastered on your face. I'm not talking about a beaming smile here. That would make you appear fake. You simply want a relaxed, engaged facial expression. You want to look as though you're being entertained.

To get your intrigued facial expression down, do the following:

Look in the Mirror

Try different expressions on for size. See which ones look engaged and which ones look fake or even annoyed. Everyone has to find the BFF that feels natural. Authenticity is the ultimate goal here, but you might have to fake it for a short time (an old one-liner) until you get it right. Truth is, what may look right to others may initially feel like a wise-aleck smirk to you. It's a closed-mouth smile. No ear-to-ear, frozen in the high-beams, toothy grins, please, lest you look like a Miss America contestant. Once you get your smile down, practice it constantly, using communication applications such as Skype and FaceTime to gauge your progress.

Look Just as Curious When You're Listening as When You're Talking

Once you stop talking, don't lose your animation and instantly transform into a sourpuss. When you suddenly break into a smile for the camera or for an audience, the smile comes off as fake. Similarly, if your smile turns into a bored frown just after speaking, your audience will suspect the smile was anything but genuine. This is especially important when you are part of a panel discussion, during which someone else has the floor. Try to lean in and look interested in what others are saying.

But Don't Become Robotic

Mitt Romney opted for the smirky-faced-robot look in the 2012 campaign, but unfortunately for him, he executed it poorly. Instead of a quarter smile, he constantly had an insipid three-quarter smile on his face. The expression was so ingrained from using it all day, every day on the campaign trail, that he showcased it whether he was looking adoringly at his wife, Ann, sitting next to him during an interview or looking at his bitterly hated political rival during a presidential debate. At that level, having a one-size-fits-all facial expression is not a wise move. The lack of variance to his expressiveness led me to call it the Stepford Smile. After a while it leaves you feeling a little creeped out. Michael Dukakis was guilty of the same thing when he ran for president in 1988. During a presidential debate against George H. W. Bush (forty-one, not forty-three), the moderator asked whether his views on capital punishment would change if his wife, Kitty, were raped and murdered. (I guarantee they don't teach that line of questioning in the Columbia University School of Journalism.) At the first hint that the question was turning to something as gruesome and unthinkable as an act of violence against his wife, the governor would have been well served by losing that dopey grin. But he didn't. In fact, he turned the exchange into a memorable gaffe by ignoring the premise of the question and starting his answer with some wonky policy message about capital punishment. I think that was the episode that prompted the comedian Mark Russell to nickname him Zorba the Clerk.

Exaggerate the BFF if You Have Facial Hair

Men with mustaches have it particularly hard. If their facial hair drapes down the sides of their mouth (Fu Manchu style), it reinforces that frowning contour of the face.

Teach Your Mouth to Relax

In addition to suffering from BRF, many people accidentally perform a myriad of problematic involuntary movements that I collectively call Busy Mouth. When people feel anxious or are concentrating, they do various things with their mouths that are anything but attractive. Some lick their lips. Some press their lips together (the motion women make after applying lipstick). Some bite their lips. Some give a quick lizardlike tongue thrust. Some do all of the above.

Busy Mouth usually kicks in after someone has finished talking. Now the mouth has to shift from lots of movement during speech to remaining calmly stationary while listening. If a stationary BFF were easy to pull off, more people would be able to do it without resorting to these Busy-Mouth motions. But it's hard, and worse yet, most of us have no idea we're even making these movements.

If you think I'm getting nitpicky here, consider the first paragraph from this *New York Times* sports column on June 18, 2013, after the Miami Heat lost a critical game in the NBA Finals: "The hour was late, the mood was grim and LeBron James was doing that weird thing with his mouth again, scrunching and gritting and swiveling the entire lower half of his face, his discomfort on full display." Avoiding Busy Mouth could be as simple as focusing on using your closed-mouth quarter smile while listening to others. It's hard to bite, lick, and purse your lips if you are smiling in an attentive and engaged way.

PITCH-PERFECT POINTER

When you make eye contact, you are communicating, "I'm paying attention." Many people, however, feel uncomfortable making eye contact; it deprives them of the mental privacy they need to be able to concentrate on what they're going to say next. That privacy is shattered when you're looking at somebody staring at you while you speak. But looking down at the carpet or up at the ceiling tiles is strictly off-limits. This makes you appear both distracted and uninterested. If you feel uncomfortable with eye contact, try this trick: stare at a man's sideburn or a woman's earring. It will give you something very small and private to focus on while you regain the capacity to concentrate, and the other person will never know that your eye contact is slightly askew.

Don't reserve your curious expression and conversational style only for high-stakes conversations. Practice them at home over dinner, in the airport while making conversation with strangers, and on the sidelines as you watch your kid play soccer. That way you'll hone your craft, and you'll be a lot less likely to be prone to off-putting facial expressions and nervous mannerisms. Eventually, with enough practice, your BFF will become your everyday face, and you'll be able to use curious questions to keep any conversation going. Once that happens, you'll be the person everyone gravitates to during the party, the very person who ensures that everyone goes home with the thought, "Wow, I had the *best* time."

9

THE DRAPER PRINCIPLE

Does anyone have any questions for my answers?
—HENRY KISSINGER

WISH EVERY SINGLE one of my clients watched AMC's hit television show *Mad Men*, about a Madison Avenue advertising agency in the early 1960s. That's because Don Draper, the show's main character, often spouts advertising advice that's nearly identical to what I tell my clients for public speaking, job interviews, media interviews, and just about all high-stakes conversational situations.

In all the seasons *Mad Men* has been on the air, one Draper mantra has risen above all others: "If you don't like what's being said, change the conversation."

He first said it when his firm was representing the developers who would be tearing down the old Pennsylvania Station in New York to construct the then-new Madison Square Garden. New Yorkers were quite attached to their majestic train station, so there was lots of opposition to the idea, with people protesting in the streets. Draper told the head of the development company that the tactic for these controversial situations was a simple one. It was to change the conversation. Take it away from the focus on what is being lost and direct it toward what's being gained: a modern, fantastic, shining new city on a hill.

DON'T IGNORE DON

Many people go into job and media interviews disregarding Don Draper's advice. Rather than steering the conversation away from areas that are not their strength, they obediently answer just the questions the interviewer asks. This is like sitting in the back of a car being taken for a joyride. Will the car end up where you want it to go? Probably not. It will more likely end up where the driver wants to go. Instead, think of this interview dynamic like a Driver's Ed car. Remember those, with the dual steering wheels?

Passively allowing others to dictate the content and flow of a discussion takes the steering wheel out of your hands, something you want to avoid. This issue pops up in a variety of important settings:

- Running a meeting or a panel discussion. One person attempts to dominate the discussion. If you let someone hijack the proceedings, you'll look completely ineffectual at controlling the situation.
- About to close a deal. One of your coworkers decides now is a great time to share her frustrations about parenting her sullen and contrary teenage daughter. You can see by the look on your client's face that this nearly done deal has a chance of coming undone if this continues too long.
- At an office brainstorming session, which several colleagues have turned into a competition to impress the boss.
- Dining with an important client who is going on and on and on about a topic that you know nothing about. You want to shift the conversation toward a topic in which you can participate, but you don't want to make the client feel as though he or she has been abruptly cut off.

Developing the skill of subtly changing the conversation can help you keep meetings running smoothly, close more deals, and get your ideas heard during brainstorming sessions.

The Draper Principle is one of the most important skills we teach clients who are preparing for media and job interviews. In these situations, you never know what kind of interviewer you'll end up with. Will it be someone cold and confrontational? If so, you'll need to make sure their sour demeanor doesn't tamp you down. Remind yourself that it's most likely the interviewer's basic personality rather than a negative response to you. But maybe your interviewer will be enthusiastic and chummy. On the surface you might think that this person would bring out the best in you. Just be careful they don't bring out too much of you. With people we like and instantly trust, we tend to reveal more and let down our guard. I always tell clients that it's the interviewers you'd like to go drinking with who should make you wariest. When you take a liking to them, you want to help them, and that might mean answering a question that's not in your best interests to take head-on. Former New York City mayor Ed Koch, a media expert, once said, "The most guileful amongst the reporters are those who appear friendly and smile and seem to be supportive. They are the ones who will seek to gut you on every occasion."

Regardless of your interviewer's demeanor, your number one priority is to stay in control of the conversation. This determination will dramatically increase your chance of success.

DRIVE THE CONVERSATION WHERE YOU NEED IT TO GO

The vast majority of people steer conversations poorly. When CNN moderator John King attempted to get presidential candidate Mitt Romney to answer the question he had posed, Romney barked, "Look, you get to ask the questions you want; I get to give the answers I want." Not a winning strategy, at least in the eyes of Mark

Twain, who once said, "Never pick a fight with people who buy ink by the barrel."

Here are some other egregious examples of poor steering.

Sticking to the Script

If you pay close attention to some politicians as they are interviewed, you'll probably find that many of them seem to deliver verbatim material. They give the same pat answers no matter the question. This technique is so prevalent that Robert McNamara said one of the things he learned as secretary of defense during the Vietnam War was "Don't answer the question you were asked. Answer the question you wish you were asked."

The Non Sequitur

Radically changing the topic of a conversation without any fluid segue is like switching from Mozart to Meatloaf midsong. It's jarring and leaves your listeners with a strange feeling.

When Todd Rogers and Michael Norton from Harvard Business School asked listeners to rate the trustworthiness of speakers, the listeners gave poor ratings to speakers who abruptly changed the topic—in this case, talking about health care when they were asked about terrorism. On the other hand, if the speaker digressed only slightly (a technique you'll learn later in this chapter), listeners often didn't notice that the question was dodged at all, and they tended to rate the speaker as trustworthy.

The Verbal Hand

I know people have been poorly media-trained when they pull this lame attempt at bridging out of their back pocket: "I'm not here to talk about that. What I am here to talk about is . . ." When you abruptly change topics like this, you are telling your interviewer and everyone who is listening, "I don't care what the question is, I'm going straight to my talking points." This is a tactic employed by third-rate politicians. It's overused, and it's clumsy. Another transparent line often used to avoid an undesirable question: "We're just really focused on . . ." That's not fooling anybody. Far better: "Sure, I could see where that might be a source of interest, but in my mind here's what really matters. . . ." This approach validates the premise of the question instead of being contrary.

Lane Weaving

Sarah Palin did this constantly, much to Tina Fey's delight. More than a few *Saturday Night Live* parodies were based on Palin's propensity for swerving from one conversational lane to another during media interviews. We now know that she didn't go with the conversational flow of traffic because she didn't have command of the material. But that's just the point. If you want to sound like an informational lightweight, veering all over the road is a sure way to do it. For instance, the ABC News anchor Charlie Gibson once asked Palin, "What insight into Russian actions, particularly in the last couple of weeks, does the proximity of [Alaska] give you?"

She answered, "They're our next-door neighbors. And you can actually see Russia from land here in Alaska, from an island in Alaska."

Gibson then pressed her to answer the question, asking, "What insight does that give you into what they're doing in Georgia?"

This time Palin swerved even more, "Well, I'm giving you that perspective of how small our world is and how important it is that we work with our allies to keep good relations with all of these countries, especially Russia.

" . . . We will not repeat a Cold War. We must have good relationship with our allies, pressuring, also, helping us to remind Russia that it's in their benefit, also, a mutually beneficial relationship for us all to be getting along."

The Stutter Step

You commit this blunder when you hesitate. You want to start talking. You open your mouth. You take a breath. You might even make a guttural noise. But you fail to actually break into the conversation. Studies by Rogers and Norton at Harvard found that listeners were likely to notice a speaker was dodging a question if the speaker stuttered. The point is, don't open your mouth to speak until you're sure that the first sound you utter is crisp, meaningful content rather than just sound, or worse yet, nothing at all. Also try to avoid having your first few words be spoken through an exhalation. This sound is closely associated with futility and frustration and makes you sound exasperated.

HOW TO TALK LIKE DON

Now you know how *not* to change the conversation. Let's get to the important part: how to steer any conversation in any direction you choose—without leaving the other participants feeling as though you've hijacked the discussion. Here are some techniques that might help:

Get Inside Your Interviewer's Head

Before heading into any Pitch-Perfect situation, think about the types of questions and topics you might encounter. What will others likely ask you? What material might your listeners want to know about? What is most likely to come up? You may not be able to prepare for every single question someone may lob in your direction, but you'll probably come close.

Anticipate the Question

In chapter 8, we discussed the importance of curious listening. Here's one of the most important reasons to get this skill down: curious listening allows you to better plan your response. What made Andy Murray so unbeatable during the historic 2013 Wimbledon Men's Final was his uncanny anticipation. By watching the racket position of his opponent before he hit the ball, Murray could start running to the spot where he knew the ball would end up. If he had waited to move until after Novak Djokovic hit the ball, he wouldn't have stood a chance.

In conversation and interviews, we often make that mistake. We wait until the other person has finished speaking before we contemplate what we're going to say. As we've already gone over while discussing the No-Tailgating Principle—thinking and talking simultaneously is a poor strategy that leads to mistakes. That's when you end up stumbling, buying time with transparent stall tactics (That's a great question!), starting off with filler talk ("Um, ah, um, I think that, um, . . ."), or responding so literally to the question that you fail to make your point.

To get a jump on where the question will go, pay close attention to the very beginning of what someone says. Before someone ever asks you a question, she or he gives you plenty of contextual cues that set up that question. You'll hear opinion or observations that relate to the question someone is going to ask many sentences later.

For instance, here's a typical interview question:

"I see you've decided to expand into Latin America. There's been a lot of speculation that companies are putting their advertising revenue into those markets. What are your thoughts about this kind of investment in Central and South America?"

Many people don't start thinking up a response until they hear the phrase "What are your thoughts?" Yet you can start planning your response as early as the words "Latin America."

By taking your cues from the first few words rather than the last few, you'll figure out the direction of the conversation early. This will give you time to think of your response long before you're asked, "What do you think about that?"

Line Up the Pitch-Perfect Triumvirate

When you develop this new skill of listening to the question with heightened attention to the first sentence or so, you will find that you can identify the topic of the question much earlier. This will allow you valuable time to answer three key questions:

1. What's my point?
2. How will I illustrate it (an example, a story, or data)?
3. What are the first five words out of my mouth?

This three-step process will keep you from rambling and meandering your way through some long-winded and redundant speech. Now just to make things more interesting, let's turn the conversation into one that you want no part of. Perhaps the discussion is moving to a controversial topic that you want to steer away from. Or maybe you've hit a conversational roadblock. The topic of conversation is one you can't relate to. You have no material and can't engage in the conversation without bluffing your way through it. This happens frequently. Recently, one of the all-news cable channels had a segment on the fact that three in five Americans admitted to trying to appear cleverer than they really are. Crazy poll, huh? But it points to the fact that many people are in over their conversational heads. That's a dangerous way to live. In the following pages, you'll find specific advice for smoothly navigating your way through those potentially perilous scenarios.

THE CONVERSATIONAL DETOUR

We often find ourselves mired in conversations that make us yearn for Harry Potter's invisibility cloak. This happened just the other night at a lovely dinner party attended by four couples, all of us friends from college. Suddenly in the midst of this tasty home-cooked meal came a tasteless remark from one of the men. He had noticed that one of our female classmates (not at the dinner) had posted pictures on Facebook at the conclusion of her 10K race.

He blurted, "Wow, have any of you checked out Cynthia's legs recently? She looks beyond great!"

I didn't have the courage to lift my eyes from my beef tenderloin for fear I might catch his poor wife shooting him the stinkeye. In the beat or two of silence that followed, everyone at the table expected the conversation to move off in another direction. But how? Anyone attempting the ole "Hey, how about those Yankees, huh?" would've gotten kicked in the shins under the table. Much to our chagrin, our friend's public display of obsession with Cynthia's form didn't stop there.

"No, I mean she practically looks better now than when we were in school! If I were her husband, I'd think about getting rid of that paunch, 'cause someone who looks that hot in a pair of shorts is a total guy magnet."

His wife was now turning the color of the roasted beets.

Steering such a conversation away to safer ground requires a deft touch. You must find the sweet spot between too radical a change of subject and contributing anything on-topic enough to prolong the tackiness. To do this, you want to master the art of widening the topic.

Take the narrow scope of the conversation and broaden it only as much as you need to in order to get away from the toxicity but still make it seem related to the topic that is being discussed.

For instance, at this dinner, I chimed in with, "Well, I think the majority of our classmates are just taking better care of themselves. I mean, my parents probably never exercised after the age of thirty. . . ." Suddenly we were now talking about the inherent differences between our parents' generation and ours—a safer, more benign subject.

This tactic is especially handy when you are about to reach a conversational dead end. For instance, if my wife is at a party and someone starts talking about the Mets, she might be at a loss. She doesn't follow the Mets (like me, she's a Yankees fan) and has nothing germane to contribute to the conversation. She can, however, broaden the topic to something that's fresh in her mind—an NPR interview she heard with R. A. Dickey, the 2012 Cy Young Award winner who at the time was on the Mets. At any point, she can steer the conversation in a different direction with, "I heard the most interesting interview the other day with R. A. Dickey and how his career was almost finished when another pitcher taught him how to throw a knuckleball." So while my wife may not know whether the Mets were in the playoff race or last place, this related knowledge keeps her active in the conversation.

Similarly, let's say you are at a dinner party and someone is talking about the craziness of the admission process for preschools—something many parents of young children obsess over in New York City. But if you're like me, your children are college age. At first glance, this is a dead-end topic for you, but you can steer the conversation wider with something like, "I gotta tell you, this kind of admissions stress will follow them for years. My daughter just had an interview to study abroad, and she was so nervous about it."

Mirroring a little of the question in your answer can help you shift from one topic to another in just a sentence or two. Sometimes it doesn't even take President Obama a full sentence to veer away from a question. Often he needs only one word. Do you know which words he relies on to avoid answering the original question so he can move on to the point he really wants to convey? One is *look*, and the other is *listen*. On paper they look imperious and condescending, almost scolding in nature. But he tries to deliver them in a tone of voice that conveys, "Let's just be frank and honest here for a minute."

THE CAMOUFLAGED CUTOFF

Few feelings in life are more helpless than losing the floor in a conversation and seeing no hope of getting it back. Sometimes standing around in a conversation cluster at an office party with the boss is a lot like a crosstalk segment on CNBC in which there are five or six guests participating all at once: it's a free-for-all, and the person who gets heard is often the one to speak up first or talk the loudest. Or maybe it happens at work in a brainstorming meeting where your colleague doesn't let you get a word in. Or perhaps you are moderating a discussion, and some egotistical panelist thinks that the time-limit rules don't apply to him. People like that seem to not even breathe, so as not to provide you with an opening. You need to break in, but you want to do it in a way that doesn't make you seem rude.

Executing a Camouflaged Cutoff is a very simple technique. You just finish the end of someone's sentence. It's exactly what old married couples do.

Chances are, there will be several opportunities where you know how someone is going to finish a thought. So finish the sentence for them and then quickly say, "It's interesting you bring that up, because that's really at the heart of another topic I want to get to. . . ." Or volley the conversation to someone else on the panel or in your conversation cluster. Try something like, "I think Susan was mentioning something related to that recently. Susan, what was it you were saying about . . . ?"

Don't be apologetic or feel as though you're being rude for interjecting. You might be talking over someone for a few words, but the trick is to not stop. It's a verbal game of chicken, and you just have to make up your mind that you are not going to relent but instead are going to make the other person yield.

This is the very technique that I taught the executive of a major PR firm that I mentioned in chapter 1. The first time I trained her, she was about to moderate a panel. Panel moderators must be able to discreetly subdue panelists who try to use up all the available oxygen in the room.

The Draper Principle is not something you need for everyday conversations. Think of it as that extra-credit work that comes in handy during those pivotal but also tense conversational moments. Practice it now so you'll be able to call on it during Q&A sessions, panel discussions, and pitch meetings—those times when results really matter.

10

HOW TO THINK ON YOUR FEET

*I've always considered myself to be just average talent and
what I have is a ridiculous insane obsessiveness for practice
and preparation.*

—WILL SMITH

'LL NEVER FORGET the day Diana Ross's superstar aura got turned
"Upside Down."

I witnessed it firsthand after my high-school alma mater hired
me to produce a video brochure to promote the school.

Diana's daughter happened to be in the graduating class that
year. As a result, Diana agreed to give the commencement speech.
I thought back to my own class's graduation. At the other end of
the celebrity spectrum, we graduating seniors listened as New York
City Council president Carol Bellamy displayed all the oratory flair
and charisma of a subway booth clerk. How could I not film Diana
Ross, the queen of Motown, for the school's video brochure? She's
the artist *Billboard* magazine declared "Female Entertainer of the
Century."

It was a glorious June day bathed in cloudless sunshine. All the
seniors, their parents, the entire faculty and alumni were gathered
on a sloping, billiard-table-green lawn overlooking the majestic
Hudson River. We were all primed for something truly special.
The Motown legend stepped up to the lectern with no notes.

"Wow," I thought. "We're about to see how a real pro does it."

Her speech was probably no more than six to seven minutes, but it felt like an hour. There was no structure, no flow, and no content. The great pop diva must have said, no fewer than half a dozen times, "I'm so sorry, this is not coming out the way I planned."

But that was just the point. She hadn't planned. And as she stepped away from the microphone, it was clear, at least to me, that even she knew that her performance had been a disappointment. Her speech clearly had been the mountain that was high enough—too high in fact.

Trust me. No matter who you are—whether you are a celebrity or an engineer, a gifted orator or just someone who's trying to get ahead at work—you don't want to ever walk in Diana's stilettos. No one wants to feel the heat of embarrassment that the pop diva must have felt that day as she was standing there in front of that audience who so desperately wanted to like what she was saying.

If you make a habit of winging it—of talking publicly without preparing ahead of time—it's just a matter of time before that happens to you. There are only so many times that magic fairy dust will come sprinkling down on you, bestowing you with instantaneous eloquence and profundity. You will have an off day, and your reliance on spontaneity will blow up in your face.

It might not happen today. It might not happen tomorrow. But it will, indeed, happen.

In chapter 6, I likened ad-libbing to driving a car on a foggy, winding mountain road. If you have ever done this, then you know it can be sheer terror not knowing whether something terrible is going to happen in the next hundred feet. At moments like those, the only thing you want to do is be able to see beyond the hood of the car. The less visibility you have, the more anxiety you feel.

The same holds true for communication. Not being sure of your next thought or even your next word is equally scary, but here's the difference: in a car, you're likely to slow down in order to minimize the likelihood of an accident. If only our instincts were that good when we're talking. Strangely, we generally do the exact opposite. The more anxiety we feel, the faster we talk.

In public speaking, the only thing worse than winging it is winging it while tailgating. This deadly combo creates fertile ground for a whole host of verbal woes: clichés, stumbles and stammers, filler words, and narratives that are meandering and pointless. Friends shouldn't let friends ad-lib when the stakes are high.

Even professionals—people who speak publicly for a living—often end up regretting their ad-libbed remarks. Consider Jodie Foster's acceptance speech for the Cecil B. DeMille Award at the 2013 Golden Globes.

So while I'm here being all confessional, I guess I have a sudden urge to say something that I've never really been able to air in public. So, a declaration that I'm a little nervous about but maybe not quite as nervous as my publicist right now, huh, Jennifer? But I'm just going to put it out there, right? Loud and proud, right? So I'm going to need your support on this.

I am single. Yes I am, I am single. No, I'm kidding—but I mean I'm not really kidding, but I'm kind of kidding. I mean, thank you for the enthusiasm. Can I get a wolf whistle or something? Jesus. Seriously, I hope you're not disappointed that there won't be a big coming-out speech tonight because I already did my coming out about a thousand years ago back in the Stone Age, in those very quaint days when a fragile young girl would open up to trusted friends and family and coworkers and then gradually, proudly to everyone who knew her, to everyone she actually met. . . .

It's amazing how someone's embarrassing performance can make you think twice about your long-held admiration and respect. I've always been a big Jodie Foster fan. She always struck me as a highly intelligent and accomplished woman, a nonconformist who did not subscribe to the same level of shallow narcissism as many of her Hollywood peers. When I heard that speech, my first thought was, "Wow, did I ever misread her!" Paying homage to Mel Gibson—another actor I once liked—toward the end of her speech probably didn't help much, either.

Somehow celebrities kid themselves, *When the red light goes on, I'll turn my magic on.* Maybe it's because none of the sycophants surrounding them have the guts to tell them to prepare and practice. All that meticulous prep that leads to oratory greatness can be just downright unglamorous.

Note to self: It's a good idea never to talk about controversial or sensitive topics—including rape, pornography, ethnic groups, politics, and religion—unless you've carefully planned your remarks ahead of time. This hasn't stopped many a celebrity, athlete, and politician. Clayton Williams lost his bid for the Texas governorship over a careless comment about rape. Even World Wrestling Entertainment fired Abraham Washington after the wrestling manager said on air during *Monday Night Raw,* "Wrestler Titus O'Neil was like Kobe Bryant at a hotel in Colorado . . . unstoppable."

Bad analogy. As was the one that Mark McKinnon, an aide to former president George W. Bush, came up with to describe Texas governor Rick Perry's brain freeze during a Republican debate. McKinnon's pitch-putrid moment was calling Perry's mishap "the human equivalent of the shuttle *Challenger.*" Don't ever compare something embarrassing with something tragic. The nation grieved over the loss of life from the *Challenger* catastrophe. To draw a parallel to Perry's mishap is stupid and disrespectful. I also advise clients to refrain from using the word *tsunami* in business to describe a massive influx of something beneficial, as in, "We've literally had a tsunami of new orders once we came out with the updated model." Hearing it used in that context strikes a sour note.

And Congressman Todd Akin came under fire when, during his run for the Senate, he was asked whether a woman who had become pregnant due to rape should have the option of abortion. He replied:

> Well you know, people always want to try to make that as one of those things, well how do you, how do you slice this particularly tough sort of ethical question. First of all, from what I understand from doctors, that's really rare. If it's a legitimate rape, the female body has ways to try to shut that whole thing down. But let's assume that maybe that didn't work or something. I think there should be some punishment, but the punishment ought to be on the rapist and not attacking the child.

I'm sure the minute Mitt Romney heard that gem, he slapped his palm against his forehead. Akin lost his bid for a Senate seat by a wide margin, but more important, it pumped some high-octane rhetorical fuel into the Democrats at a key stage of the election. Profoundly stupid spur-of-the-moment remarks are like a nuclear power plant emergency: it's nearly impossible to contain the damaging fallout.

PITCH-PERFECT POINTER

The more experienced and accomplished a public speaker you become, the more you'll be tempted to shortchange your prep. But just about any high-level performer will tell you, "You play the way you practice." If you bring an intensity and keen attention to detail in rehearsal, you'll be better able to nail the actual performance. If you just go through the motions and mail it in during your practice sessions, then you have nothing to replicate when you're doing it for real. Practice, practice, practice. And when in doubt, practice one more time.

SPONTANEITY IS ANOTHER WORD FOR REGRET

So often in my training sessions, the first thing I write on a white-board is the word *spontaneity*. Then I circle it and put a big thick line through it. Don't do it. Sure, you may get a buzz from living close to the edge, but you will live to regret it.

Some people bristle when I tell them that for all their love of spontaneity, spontaneity doesn't love them back. "It's fun," they tell me. "I like to show I can think on my feet. Who wants to be some programmed automaton? That's boring! Besides, it isn't possible to practice for everything, is it?"

By no means am I suggesting that you be messaged and re-hearsed 24/7. But on any given day, each of us has a handful of Pitch-Perfect situations in which there's absolutely no reason to wing anything. It could be an update you have to give to your boss, a call with a potential client, an evaluation you have to give to your assistant during an employment review, or a conversation with one of your children on a matter of importance. The emotions and pressures associated with each one of those can prevent you from thinking clearly. Having an outline of how you're going to make your point and use Pitch-Perfect techniques to communicate sensitive information is the best insurance policy I know to avoid later saying, "I wish I had thought to say this."

PITCH-PERFECT POINTER

When you feel the urge to go off-script during a high-stakes situation—for instance, let's say you have a sudden urge to share a joke you heard earlier in the day—imagine the other person looking at you stone-faced, worse than not amused, with a "WTF are you talking about?" expression. Pause, then resume with your game plan.

We've all lamented, "If only I hadn't said that." Or mused, "If I had it to do over again, here's what I should have said." These regrets typically follow impromptu moments when you felt on the spot and didn't have any material at the ready. Like suddenly standing next to your boss at the office holiday party? Was it filled with *ums, ahs,* filler, and general awkwardness?

You can try to chalk that up to nerves, but really it's a simple lack of planning. Let's be honest. Should you really be surprised at the prospect of being in a conversation cluster with the boss at an office function? I don't think so. It's a given. Consider putting in some prep time as a career insurance policy. You may not end up needing it, but you never want to need it and not have it. This is a classic situation in which saying the first thing that pops into your head could be a career killer.

You would probably do a little bit of research in advance of an important client meeting. So why not do some for an encounter that is ten times more important? This is an opportunity to demonstrate that there's more to you than what your boss sees at work or hears about you from others.

Here's a simple strategy: stay current with your boss's interests, hobbies, and family milestones. Did she just have an op-ed published in the newspaper or a blog on HuffPo? Is he a huge college basketball fan? Did her daughter just get her MBA? Each one of these represent solid conversation starters:

1. "So I imagine you've been up late this week watching the NCAAs, given that your alma mater is in the Sweet Sixteen."
2. "I read your post this week on the need for more diversity on corporate boards of directors. That's such an important message to get out there."
3. "Congratulations. I heard your daughter just graduated from business school. You must be very proud. What is she interested in pursuing?"

So now you've broken the ice in the best way possible: teeing the boss up to talk about something that makes him or her feel good. Now what? What will separate you from the pack is being an equal in the conversation, instead of some lapdog flunky brown-nosing like there's no tomorrow. You also don't want everything that comes out of your mouth to be a question. Playing the role of interviewer just makes the boss feel as though he or she is at work, or worse yet, getting grilled by a reporter.

To hold your own, you need to know a thing or two about the topic you've just raised. Come with an observation from something interesting you read or saw. If you're halfway decent at it, it'll probably take you all of thirty seconds to find something pertinent.

So for the basketball fan, try something like, "I read an interesting profile of the head coach recently in the *New Yorker*, and I was fascinated to learn that . . ." That's a better way to go than, "Did you happen to see the profile of the head coach in the *New Yorker* last week?" Try never to put bosses on the spot like that and force them to admit you've done something they haven't. You want to be an intellectual challenge without overtaking them, the same way you'd want to make sure you lost to them by one or two strokes if you were playing golf together.

For scenario number two, you'd take the same approach. "I saw this documentary last week that compared two companies—one that was very diverse and one that was completely one-dimensional. The findings were really interesting. . . ."

For scenario number three, keep it positive. The last thing you want to do is cite some article you read that stated that this crop of MBAs was more likely to be unemployed than any in recent history. That's not how you want to demonstrate how well informed you are, by bumming people out.

Be prepared to be asked for your opinion. Have something solid, not wishy-washy, but don't come across rigid and closed-minded.

Having a conversational template like this can help you avoid putting your foot in your mouth. And if you're shy, there's an extra benefit: it gives you something to say. It takes the pressure off of having to be engaging on the spur of the moment. The less pressure you feel, the more articulate you're likely to be.

This is just one example of many. In reality, there are few if any speaking situations that you can't prepare for ahead of time. I've also been hired to help clients with winning strategies when someone at an event unexpectedly whispers in their ear, "Hey, would you mind getting up and saying a few words?" Speaking on short notice can be nerve-racking, but surprisingly, there's even a way to prepare for this.

PITCH-PERFECT POINTER

What do you do if that bacterial organism known as your office nemesis breaks into an important conversation and attempts to steal the floor? Steer the conversation to a topic that you and the person to whom you were originally speaking have a connection. You shouldn't overtly exclude such persons and make it obvious that you are shutting them down. You should just give them less opportunity. If they do try to insinuate themselves into the conversation, it will seem desperate on their part. For instance, say you and the boss were at a company outing and the other person wasn't there. Maybe you initiate a discussion about that outing or about something that predated the other person's joining the company.

STORIES TO NAIL DOWN NOW

Most of your conversational repertoire should come in the form of a story. And here's the great part: stories are more enjoyable and natural for us to convey than the typical elevator pitch—and they also keep your listener far more engaged.

Even brainless chitchat at a party is an opportunity for you to toss in some storytelling. Spend some time right now considering the main types of stories that you'll want to have at the ready for any spontaneous speaking situation.

The Standing-with-a-Drink-in-Your-Hand Stories

Think of stories that illustrate the answers to the usual questions that people generally ask. In the following section, you'll find common networking questions along with the stories I personally have at the ready.

YOU HAVE KIDS?

"Yes. We have three, ages twenty-one, twenty, and nineteen." And given that answer, I brace myself for the ensuing tacky response, "Well you certainly don't believe in taking a breather do you?" That's a quip I never directly reply to. "It's had its advantages over the years, since everyone's usually interested in seeing the same movies and doing the same activities on vacation" is what I typically say. I never whine or complain to strangers or even acquaintances.

WHERE ARE YOU FROM?

"Born and raised in New York City and except for a year and a half stint in Washington, DC, I have never lived anywhere else. But I have made it to forty-eight states." That last line usually sparks curiosity as to how I've managed to get around so much, and also, which two states are missing. (In case you are curious: Idaho and North Dakota.)

WHAT DO YOU DO FOR A LIVING?

I often say, "I'm a communications coach. So if you were an author or a musician being interviewed on TV about your new work, or a corporate executive about to give a TED Talk, or a celebrity about to go public with a personal crisis, I would be the person who prepares you to say the right things in order to enhance your public image." It's short, but it gives three different and distinct examples, something I call the spectrum answer. The idea is to cast the net far and wide in terms of what you do so you increase the possibility of others discovering a need to do business with you in the future.

DO YOU LIKE IT?

This question opens a trap many people fall into: incessant belly-aching about their job. Nobody wants to hear that. It's better to focus on one positive element from that experience and instead talk about your true aspirations or what you would like to do next. For instance, when people ask me how I felt about working for ABC, I say, "I owe an enormous debt of gratitude to that network for igniting the entrepreneurial side of me and making it possible for me to start my own company." Doesn't that sound so much better than, "By that point in my career, I'd just had it with TV, and I was at odds with the direction the show was taking"?

HOW DID YOU GET INTO DOING WHAT YOU DO?

"I was a reporter and producer for twenty-five years in TV and might still be doing that today if it hadn't been for one woman's advice back in 2000." And then I tell the story of the video shoot that sparked my coaching business that I shared with you in the introduction to this book.

The Aha Story.

This is the one I just referred to, and everyone should have one. It's about a pivotal moment in time when something dawned on you and you came to an important realization about work, family life, or something else. A good story often recalls the exact moment when we made a crucial decision, experienced an important revelation, or decided to roll the dice and go for it.

The Current Event

And finally, closely follow one story in the news and have an opinion about it, preferably one that isn't disrespectful to others' dissenting opinions. It should be a topic that has nothing to do with you. Scan the newspaper every morning and become familiar with at least one current event that others might find interesting. Then when you find yourself standing on line at the Starbucks near the office with a colleague, you can spark a conversation slightly more provocative than "Wassup? How's it goin'?" "How about that guy who won the Power Ball. Did you hear a family court judge has already attached part of his winnings because he's been behind on his child-support payments for several months?"

If you have these stories at the ready, you'll rarely, if ever, feel the sudden urge to ad-lib. But you're still not done. You also want to have a few lines prepared to help you open and close any Pitch-Perfect conversation.

KNOW YOUR OPENER

I'm always amazed by how much thought people will put into what to say during an important pitch meeting, but how little thought they put into how they will break the ice. Most people leave the initial greet and handshake up to chance. They wing it, and they miss an important opportunity to seal the deal.

If your icebreaker goes well, you will have paved the way to nailing the account long before you've ever started your pitch. On the other hand, a poor, awkward icebreaker means you're going to have to work that much harder just to get back to even. Now the actual presentation better be great. Why add to what's already substantial pressure?

To break the ice, play three degrees of separation. Just about all of us can find something in common with nearly everyone we come into contact with. The only thing that separates you from the person you want to win over is knowledge. So come armed with it. Research anyone you plan to meet for business in just the same way you would research a potential date. Hardly anyone goes on a date these days without running a social media background check. Do the same for your business prospects. Know their bios. Google them. Check out their Facebook pages and LinkedIn profiles. View their Twitter streams.

If you look hard enough, you will find something in common. Years ago I was hired to media-train the commissioner of one of the major sports leagues. After poking around the Web for five to ten minutes, I discovered that he played high-school football for a school very close to mine in the same exact year. It gave me the opportunity to talk about how closely our high-school sports lives mirrored each other's and what a shame it was that we were so close but never actually played against each other.

If you're lucky, you don't even need to search for your common denominator. Earlier this year, I was hired to work with a famous actress, someone who, I'd learned from her agent, thought that the media-training session with me was nothing but a waste of time. "I'm just warning you," said the agent, "she's already announced to me that she's going to arrive late and leave early. So good luck with this one!"

I knew I had to win her over within the first few seconds of conversation, or otherwise the entire training session would be awkward and unproductive. Fortunately, I had one degree of separation, and it was a damn good one. Almost thirty years ago, I had worked for a female executive in TV news whom this actress later portrayed in a movie. This actress was researching her role and shooting the movie at exactly the same time I was working in this news bureau. So after the initial shaking of hands, I said, "We have an interesting biographical overlap. At the same time you were getting inside the head of this character, I was working for her."

A genuine smile beamed across her face and the next thing I knew, we were deep into a conversation about the state of television news, our degree of separation now far in the rearview mirror. It was an opportunity to show this accomplished actress that I wasn't just some hack consultant and shallow theorist who was going to subject her to Media Training 101. To my delight and amazement, she actually took notes during the training and turned out to be a lovely, genuine person. While it's enormously beneficial to do this kind of legwork ahead of time, never, ever make the other person feel as though you've digitally strip-searched them. Be subtle about it, and stick to one pertinent, fun detail rather than showing off that you know every little thing about someone's life. The goal is to get the other person feeling relaxed in dealing with you. That's not going to happen if you come across as a creepy stalker. So the following should never cross your lips prior to or during a client meeting:

"I spent a lot of time on Facebook last night checking out your Timeline."

"Wow! It's amazing how many hits come up on Google during a search on you."

"Those pictures of you and your kids on Instagram are so cute."

PITCH-PERFECT POINTER

Industry conferences are breeding grounds for mind-numbing conversations and awkward moments. Perhaps you've gotten caught up in one. You see a colleague that you haven't seen in a year. You strike up a conversation in the hall. Soon you're staring at one another, both thinking, *How do I extricate myself from this?*

The trick to surviving such conversations is in channeling your inner David Petraeus. No, don't sleep with your biographer! Have a full battle plan drawn up in advance, with a clear idea of your opening salvo as well as your exit strategy. Brush up on news stories, commentaries, or even books that may have been written recently on your industry. For instance, if you are at an authors conference, you might mention the latest news about a publisher that is wrangling with Amazon or another large bookseller. Start off the conversation and then ask for someone's opinion.

KNOW YOUR CONVERSATIONAL ENDER

Your conversational ender can be just as important as your opener. It doesn't need to be elaborate. Often just one or two lines will do. Somewhere between rude and abrupt and apologetically self-effacing, there's an effective middle ground. You learned several when you read about the Curiosity Principle. In addition to any of those, you can recognize that the person you are talking to is important. Acknowledge that his or her time is valuable, and perhaps refer to the next time you are going to see each other and mention that you're looking forward to it. It could sound something like:

"Listen, I know you have a ton of people to mingle with and touch base with, so I just wanted to say hi. It's been so great talking to you, and I know we're going to see each other at this off-site next week. Maybe we can catch up again there."

HOW TO MAKE A QUICK CONVERSATIONAL EXIT

Sometimes a conversation turns so downright uncomfortable that the only option is to flee. If you've ever found yourself on a break at work with some people who are bad-mouthing a colleague in the office, you know what I mean. You don't want to fuel gossip or behind-the-back trashing, but you also don't want to be complicit in your silence. Abruptly walking away isn't a great option, either. Nor is saying, "You know, we really shouldn't talk about Ron this way behind his back." That comes off as holier than thou.

Try this option next time. Point out the attributes of the person who is being trashed, and then politely duck out. For instance, you might say, "Say what you will about Ron, but he's one of the guys here you can count on to . . ."

Another time you might need a quick exit is when another co-worker is pumping you for information on circulating rumors. Maybe layoffs are imminent, a management change is coming, or even a company merger or takeover is looming. Say something like, "Yeah, I know, the speculation is pretty intense . . . like you, I don't have any special knowledge of what's going on. I'm just hearing what you're hearing." Then be disciplined in keeping your mouth shut.

Then there's the chain-gang scenario, in which you are actually trapped for a long flight or an extended car ride sitting next to a client. In this situation, silence is a much better strategy than nonstop talking. Be intuitive. Read other people's body language. Don't be so wrapped up in your own head that you miss the warning signs that the other person needs a break. If your boss pulls out a stack of paperwork and you keep droning on, you can bet that your boss is thinking, "When will John shut up already?" Cut the conversation short. Say, "Listen, I'm sure you've got plenty of work to do, so don't let me keep you from it.'"

SPECIFIC ADVICE FOR SPECIFIC SITUATIONS

Plenty of uncomfortable, put-you-on-the-spot scenarios present themselves in our daily lives that require a game plan if we want to emerge unscathed. In the following pages, I'll provide detailed advice for specific high-stakes situations where you have to speak on short notice—and how to prepare for each ahead of time.

You're Asked for Your Opinion

Let's say your boss wheels around and asks you for your opinion on something out of the clear blue. The hair on the back of your neck stood at attention just reading that, didn't it? Talk about a high-stakes game! Lurking just beneath the surface of such a request lies an intimidating imperative: "Dazzle me!"

Such a situation may not present itself often, so you want to nail it when it does. Part of nailing it lies in being prepared. And let's be honest. If you're in a conference room with your boss for a meeting in which you know the agenda ahead of time, is there anything you could be asked that truly blindsides you? Map out in advance what you would offer if asked.

The quickest way to blow this opportunity is to serve up a tepid response that makes it painfully obvious that you're hedging your bets just so you can't be blamed for saying the wrong thing. Sycophants in the workplace are a dime a dozen, a club in which you don't want membership. While the suck-ups may provide a fleeting jolt of pleasure to the boss, like eating a candy bar, it never sits too well after the ego/sugar rush is gone.

Plus, if your boss seeks out your opinion, you can be sure that's exactly what your boss wants. Your boss doesn't want to waste time hearing about every possible opinion. He or she sincerely wants to know what *you* think. If you find yourself saying, "but on the other hand . . ." you're already cooked. Playing it safe when the boss has swung the door wide open for you to go for it is about as offensive to him or her as overt ass kissing.

So take a position and be prepared to back it up with some concrete examples. Do this even if you worry that your boss isn't going to agree. It's better to have a firm opinion and back it up than to have wishy-washy content conveyed through a hesitant delivery.

If you offer your opinion and it becomes quickly evident that your boss thinks the exact opposite, don't cave in and start back-pedaling at warp speed. The worst thing you could do is make it seem as though you were somehow misunderstood and that "what I really meant" was exactly what the CEO thinks. Instead start with something like, "I can totally understand that that is the prevailing view at the executive level. I'm merely offering another way of looking at it." If your boss starts to make a big deal about your disagreeing, an appropriate follow-up could be, "I realize I'm going against the majority here, but I know we have a culture that values a diversity of opinion, so I just figured I'd offer that."

You're Asked to Give a Few Words

I have a client in Washington, DC, who feels comfortable in just about every communication opportunity. He's good as a commentator on TV. He feels at ease delivering a speech at a function. He has no problem addressing his staff at an all-hands meeting. But there is one scenario that makes him get sweaty and dry-mouthed. Being asked to get up and say a few impromptu words sends him into a panic attack. I'm sure he's not alone.

Always, *always* plan for this terrifying possibility.

You may be called on to "say a few words" only 5 percent of the time, but it's one of the best public-speaking contingencies you could ever have. Because you never know when it's coming or what occasion it will fall on, the best I can do is give a strategic roadmap:

- If the event is honoring someone, decide on a personal story about that person ahead of time.
- If the event is about a special cause, plan on telling a story about how you came to be involved in the first place—what inspired you to be part of it.
- And keep it clean.

You've Just Been Ambushed

I opened this book with a story of the time I ambushed a convicted felon as he walked to his car. Fortunately, most of us will never have questions hurled at us like grenades from some microphone-wielding pit bull.

But many other situations can certainly feel like an ambush. Maybe you've just finished a presentation and your nemesis, the one who's always trying to trip you up, starts grilling you about material you haven't prepared. Or maybe you're addressing share-holders, and one of them starts hammering you for facts and stats that you don't have at the ready.

What do you do? Consider the following.

DO . . .

Prepare to talk about the hot-button issues.

Every industry has what I call third-rail topics, areas of controversy that in reality may not be that controversial but somehow take on a life of their own. In the food industry, it's obesity; in tech, it's pri-vacy; in fashion media and modeling, it's airbrushing and anorexia. If there's a toxic topic out there, you're kidding yourself if you think people outside your company haven't tapped into it.

So don't wait until you are blindsided to think of how you will respond when someone ambushes you and attempts to hang your dirty laundry for all the world to see. Come up with your responses now—and take them beyond just vague key messages and talking points. Cite specific examples and/or data that back up your de-fense. It's quite dramatic how quickly aggressors wilt under the heat of specific content.

Create the appearance that you want to talk.

Do this even if you actually won't be divulging information. You want to make it seem as if you would love to tell your side of the story but that the decision is out of your hands. For instance, if I were advising the felon I mentioned in the introduction about how to handle our encounter, I would have told him to say this: "As much as I would like to speak with you, because I am certain we have a persuasive and compelling case, I've been strictly forbidden by the lawyers to speak publicly. Now if you'd like to give me your name and contact information, I'd be happy to reach out and schedule something with you once I'm given the green light to speak about it. Until then, my hands are tied. I'm sorry. I know that doesn't help you much right now in that you have a job to do, but those are the rules I have to abide by, at least for the time being."

Shift the focus to something greater than you or your company. When people grill you, they are often searching for a personal fault. Your answer must be about more than just you. You want to make it sound as if what you or your company is doing is standard practice. For instance, not long ago, I coached an executive from a high-end kitchen-goods store. I knew that this store sold goods in Asia for 40 percent more than they do here and that this was likely to come up during interviews, so I grilled the executive about it, helping her to craft an answer to the question, "Wow, how are your consumers in China taking this? Aren't they annoyed that they have to pay 40 percent more for the exact same product?"

I coached her to start off her answer with this: "With any global company, it's a pretty standard practice to have a tiered pricing system for different regions. So let me give you a sense of how we go about setting our pricing." That way, it was no longer just about her and her company. It was about all global companies. Here are some other phrases that might work:

- "No matter what Fortune 500 company you are, these kinds of pressures are just going to present themselves from time to time."

- "Most middle managers would tell you that this a challenge we're all working to find more effective answers to."
- "It's important to keep in mind some of the trends that are affecting the entire industry."

Shift from negative wording to positive wording.

When I coached the executive from the high-end kitchen store, I suggested she shift from using the expression *more expensive* to the less off-putting *high-end*. Here are some other phrases, with suggestions on turning them from negative to either neutral or positive.

If we're *worried* about any sector, it would be . . .	We remain *cautious* in our approach to . . .
Losing these executives *hurt* us competitively.	When talented people *move on*, you have to make an *adjustment*.
We take an *aggressive* stance in our dealings with business partners.	We are *assertive* and *vocal* when we think our input can improve the outcome.
As an organization, we tend to move somewhat *slowly* on these decisions.	Historically we have benefited greatly from being *thorough* and *thoughtful* in our decision making.
To stay competitive, we're playing a bit of *catch-up*.	Based on changes we've made, we expect to *gain* market share in the near future.

DON'T . . .

Run away.

It makes you seem guilty.

Be belligerent.

The person I ambushed should have been conciliatory and empathetic to take the wind out of my sails, so then I'd look like an unreasonable jerk for continuing to press him on the issue.

Pretend to answer a question.

Be upfront and honest by saying something like, "Rather than giving you something off the top of my head, I'd rather give you something more informed and thoughtful. So why don't I follow up with you later in the day?"

Refute a negative by repeating the toxic words.

Doing so merely reinforces the negative, even though you are saying that it's not the case. In the introduction of this book, I mentioned Richard Nixon's famous blunder when he said, "I am not a crook." The word *crook* should never have crossed Nixon's lips.

This discipline is especially important in these attention-deficient times. We watch and listen to other people with such fragmented focus that the likelihood for misinterpreting what was really said is higher than it's ever been. Had Nixon refuted that notion today on TV, no doubt most of us would have been simultaneously immersed in our "second screens," the TV serving as glorified background noise. This dynamic makes it easy for us to think we heard something we didn't. "Did Nixon just say he was a crook? OMG!" Next thing you know, you're Facebook posting or tweeting that to the masses. Now all your friends and followers, who weren't watching and got the news anecdotally from you, are spreading that rumor further. That's why you don't repeat negative words. Too many things can go wrong.

So how do you get around this? Instead of repeating the negative and talking about *what it's not*, always talk about *what it is*. Be affirmative and declarative from word one and never look back. Consider how the following messages can be inverted.

Refuting the Negative	Accentuating the Positive
I am not a crook.	I have amassed a long distinguished career of public service that has been driven by one guiding principle: doing the right thing at all costs.
We're not dour, depressed people.	We are experienced professionals who fully understand that there will be times when you're tested . . . and emerging from those times with greater strength and resolve can be rewarding.
What we are doing is not spin-doctoring or some PR gimmick.	We have only one goal here: to share the information we have quickly and accurately.

Your Coworker Behaved Inappropriately

For something that happens with alarming regularity, it's still something that is shocking as hell. Hopefully, you'll never be put in that position, but if you are, have something ready to go in your back pocket. A Taser would be nice, but I was thinking more along the lines of an effective response.

I'm not talking about cases of overt harassment. Those should be met with zero tolerance and a quick trip to the head of HR. I'm talking about a gray area, a remark that flirts with stepping over the line into inappropriate but stops just short. It makes you feel uncomfortable, but you're questioning whether the offense is all in your own head.

Shutting something like that down right away can de dicey, especially if it's with someone whom you see every day and possibly work next to. How do you firmly discourage that behavior but stop short of poisoning the well? It's a delicate balancing act for sure; what you say and how you say it can make all the difference.

"Roger, . . . I know you're way too smart a guy to be lighting a match to something so dangerous. I think a safer distance would be wise."

"Gee, . . . and here I thought all this time it was my professionalism and smarts you admired. How about you just make that the focus of your admiration?"

"I have a policy of never engaging in a conversation that I wouldn't feel comfortable having my spouse overhear. This one falls into that category."

"The dynamics of this office are complicated enough. I don't think we need to add to them by wading into these waters."

"Oh, Sean. Hitting on me is so predictable. You don't want to be some walking cliché do you?"

The One Thing That You Never Could Have Expected to Go Wrong Just Went Wrong

Some of what I teach my clients is what I learned the hard way from mistakes in my own presentations—precautions to take that never occurred to me until it was too late. Spoiler alert: if you are giving a presentation from your own laptop, always turn off your airport or wireless function.

One Monday morning I was invited to present to a group at the talent agency William Morris Endeavor. All was going smoothly, and I was four or five slides into what I thought was a killer presentation when all of a sudden the unthinkable happened. Without any warning, my laptop connected to the WME wireless network. Next thing you know, all my e-mail alerts from the night before start popping up in the lower right corner of the screen, and all the really choice spam, too, like ED drug sales and other sex-life-enhancement offers. I am now convinced that my audience is no longer focused on my public-speaking tips but instead on why I might be on these mailing lists.

It took every ounce of self-control not to lunge for the laptop and yank out the cord connecting the laptop to the projector. In horrifying moments like these, just behave as though somebody's holding you at gunpoint—no sudden moves or it's curtains. So despite my DEFCON Level 5 panic, I tried to follow my own advice, which is to slow everything down and never look frazzled. Somehow I mustered a laugh (God knows where that came from) and slowly moved to the laptop to quit just my e-mail application. Figuring that this was a good teaching moment, I told them that this was the ultimate reminder that you can never get too good to be humbled or learn something in the world of public speaking. I then went for a laugh by saying, "How I got on those Viagra mailing lists I have no idea!"

If you can outwardly shrug off a mistake and make it look as though you're not the slightest bit fazed, chances are your audience will not feel anxious for you.

Wouldn't you know it, the very next week I was at Facebook headquarters in Palo Alto for a coaching session when I had a quasi déjà vu. My own computer wasn't even turned on. I was using the conference-room computer, but my Facebook account was projected on a massive screen. I was reviewing with Randi Zuckerberg (Mark's sister) some of her on-air interviews with tech guests, when my niece Olivia sent me a Facebook message that popped up on the screen: "Hey Uncle Billy, when are you going to get busy making me a batch of pesto?" The only thing that spared me from experiencing PTSD was the fact that everyone in the room laughed and thought it was cute. At a moment like that, don't even let your mind entertain the thought of how bad it could have been.

Ultimately, the more familiar you are with what you will say in both anticipated and unexpected situations, the more at ease you will be. I hope you know that I'm not advocating that you be Pitch Perfect all the time. Life would be pretty boring if you had to be. Instead, be spontaneous as long as the personal and professional stakes aren't high. Life's low-key situations (and thank goodness there are plenty of them) are the perfect opportunities to try out new conversational material for the first time. Your closest friends and family aren't likely to hold it against you if you're slightly off-pitch.

11

THE SEVEN PRINCIPLES AT WORK

Don't find fault, find a remedy; anybody can complain.
—HENRY FORD

WHEN I LOOK back on the years I worked in television, what makes me proudest is not the Emmys or the accolades. It's that my colleagues trusted me to help them solve their problems, both personal and professional. They would swing by my office, poke their heads in my doorway and ask, "You got a minute?" It wasn't long before the sofa in my office came to be called the shrink's couch. The only thing missing was Lucy's PSYCHIATRY 5¢ sign from the *Peanuts* comic strip posted on my office door. To this day, media training clients will sometimes look around the warm, relaxed setting of the Clarity Media Group offices and remark, "I feel as though I'm in my therapist's office." My frequent reply is, "In some ways you are."

Many of my former colleagues wanted help navigating delicate situations: delivering bad news, admitting a mistake and rectifying it, managing a contentious relationship with a rival colleague, responding to personal-relationship challenges. You name it, they asked. It seemed that no matter the specifics of my advice, the basic equation was the same: Fairness + Honesty + Empathy = Good Outcome.

The empathy piece is huge. The value of getting outside our

own heads and understanding how a problem looks to the other person cannot be overestimated. But it often went beyond just recognizing where the other person was coming from. Actually validating another person's position, even if counter to your own, was often a powerful part of the mix as well, as were the Seven Principles of Persuasion.

In the pages ahead, you'll find advice for navigating your way through many sticky situations, as well as for the most common communication issues my clients have encountered. I'm a big fan of these Seven Principles of Persuasion because they relate to nearly every issue you could possibly face.

HOW DO I PART WAYS WITH A BUSINESS ASSOCIATE WITHOUT BURNING A BRIDGE?

At some point in your career, I predict that, at least once, you will find yourself thinking, *I just can't work with this person!* Maybe you've already come to that realization more than once. It might have happened after your boss paired you with the office slacker and asked you both to finish a time-consuming project by Friday. Or maybe you agreed to work with a colleague on a presentation, only to realize halfway through that your colleague was too egotistical and stubborn to actually collaborate.

Perhaps it's even dicier: You own a business together and your business partner is displaying the business acumen of a fourteen-year-old.

Whatever the situation, no matter how tempting it may be to say exactly what's on your mind, never part ways by eviscerating the other person. As Tom Flynn, a talented producer at CBS News taught me years ago, you always meet people twice in this business, once on the way up and again on the way down. And because spurned people have long memories, you want to part ways gently and without drama if possible. To successfully do this, you *don't* want:

- The other person to see this as a rejection.
- To hint that there's something wrong with his or her skills or personality.
- To make any allusions about your being better off without them.

It's tempting to break up by using a clichéd phrase like, "We're just not a good fit." That's the business equivalent of saying "It's not you, it's me." It's so overused that anyone who hears that line can read between the words and guess that you really mean, "I can't stand you. It's actually not me. It's totally you."

Look for words that don't sound personal, that compliment the other person, and that allude to a future where you are both better off. You want your business associate to see how great business can be *without* you.

To do so, think about the following questions: Can you bring this up in a way that doesn't explicitly blame your business associate? Does your business associate possess a skill, personality, or talent worth complimenting? How will the future be better off for each of you if you part ways?

Consider the following examples:

The Impersonal Opening	The Compliment	The Sell
Our strengths are too similar.	You're incredibly accomplished at the creative side of the business. The only problem with that is, I'm not a good balance to you.	We would both gain a lot by working with others who have complementary and different skills.

The Impersonal Opening	The Compliment	The Sell
We're overlapping too much in what we bring to the table.	When I see how good you are at closing the deal with new clients, I often think how much further you could go with someone who could execute the business. We basically have two tablesetters and no one to serve the meal.	It's better that we address this now than five years down the road when we're stuck with no prospects for growth.
It seems we have different long-term goals.	You have such a strong vision on where to take this company that you don't need someone like me being a barrier to decision making.	Wouldn't it be great if you could make important life decisions without checking with a combative person like me?

Once you think you've got your breakup speech down, test it out on yourself. If your business associate said the same words to you, how would you feel? Would you be sold or feel betrayed by their insincerity?

Several years ago, a former colleague from my television days began stalking me to have a drink. It went on for weeks, and it was a safe assumption that he wasn't insisting on getting together just to congratulate me on breaking free of his network's tyranny. I suspected he might be looking to couple his caboose to our firm.

I didn't want to take him on for a variety of reasons, not the least of which was my total lack of respect for him when he'd been my boss at the networks. His feedback on the stories we produced was about as helpful as the emperor's critique of Mozart's operas in *Amadeus*: "Simply too many notes."

Even though it would have been sweet revenge for how poorly he treated me years earlier, when I finally agreed to meet him for drinks, I was determined not to humiliate him.

In a rather immodest way, he suggested it would generate a publicity bonanza for Clarity Media Group if he joined us. "There would be headlines in *Variety*, *PR Week*, the works," he said.

A realistic assessment of his own importance has never been his strength.

I took a deep breath. "I'm really flattered that you see our firm as the kind of place you'd like to be," I began, "but I don't know where I want to take the company right now. I have this nice little business and am totally comfortable with its current size. It's possible that at some point down the road I'll want to expand, but I can't say I'm ready to make that call at this point."

That response made it about my business and my decision not to add another position, rather than about him, his skills, and my distaste for him personally and professionally. It was clearly not the response he was looking for because, when the check came, it sat on the table equidistant between us for an uncomfortably long time. Minutes went by with no one initiating even the slightest reach for it. When it became clear that I was prepared to wait there all night if necessary, his eyes motioned to the check. "So, does this qualify as an official Clarity Media Group marketing meeting?" I remember thinking, *I'll be damned if I'm going to pick up the check after it was he who hounded me to schedule the meeting.* My verbal response to his question was simple and curt: "Not really."

Then came the true jaw-dropper from this former TV executive whose monthly Barneys clothing bill probably exceeds my annual mortgage payments: "OK, then. Let's split it." Word to the wise: only if you want to position yourself as the last man on earth to be offered a job should you insist on going Dutch on a $35 check. Bad form, bad judgment.

HOW DO I REPRIMAND EMPLOYEES WHILE KEEPING THEM MOTIVATED?

Communicating a delicate, sensitive, or unwelcome message to someone is the ultimate high-wire act. Too much diplomacy and subtlety might result in your message not coming through. If that happens, nothing changes and you don't achieve your results. Position it too bluntly and aggressively, and the recipient winds up wounded, defensive, and incapable of seeing the merit in your point.

How do you find the rare middle ground between those two extremes?

First, here's what you don't want to do. Don't . . .

- Initiate the conversation with "We need to talk." When your ninth-grade infatuation broke up with you, he or she probably started off by saying that, so the negative associations are strong and immediately make your employee brace for battle.
- Make yourself the benchmark with the phrase, "When I was your age." The minute you say that, your employee is thinking, *Listen, old man, what happened back in the day has zero relevance now.* Your employees will associate you with nagging parents.
- Mention anything about "paying dues." Sure, you might have worked twelve-hour days to get to where you are, but you can't assume your employees have the same drive and aspirations. Your success story isn't as motivating as you might think.

To turn this problem employee around, blend empathy with concern for his or her well-being. To do so, start off with an empathetic question. Wait for the answer. Then offer the reason for your concern. Use the following chart for ideas and inspiration.

Question	Reason
Is everything OK outside of work?	You seem a little distracted at work, as if you are only 60 percent here.
Is your workload manageable?	You seem anxious and stressed, and that's having an effect on others at the office.
Are you unhappy here?	When you walk through the door in the morning, you look as though this is the last place you want to be. I know it can be easy for us to lose sight of the vibe we're giving off, but I'm not the only one at work who's noticed.

You may even need more finesse than that, depending on the sensitivity of the situation. Maybe your employee's personal grooming or hygiene is noticeably bad. Or maybe they have a personality tic that others find annoying.

That's when you need to connect the smaller sensitive issue to something bigger that is in your employee's best interest. Acknowledge your employee's strengths, even as you are mentioning the issue in question. You want to make it absolutely clear that you are an ally and not an adversary. Your employee has to believe that you're on his or her side and that you are bringing this up only for his or her benefit and not because you stubbornly stick to some arbitrary notion of how things should be. As in so many scenarios, this can't come across as "I'm right and you're wrong." Put yourself in the role of mentor rather than boss. If your employee is convinced of that, then he or she will be more open and receptive to what you have to say.

That's exactly what I would have done if I'd faced a sticky issue my wife brought up recently over dinner with a few friends. She told us all about a communications quandary at the college where she is a professor. One of her colleagues teaches a course in which a student arrives every day for class not wearing shoes. While the professor found this repulsive, she was reluctant to confront the student for fear her objections would be taken the wrong way and alienate the student. And unless there was something in the university charter prohibiting bare feet in class, the professor worried that she could find herself embroiled in controversy for impinging on the student's freedom-of-expression right to dress however she likes. These days, saying the wrong thing the wrong way doesn't just start an argument, it can trigger a lawsuit.

Around the table we went, gauging how each of us would handle the situation, with only one goal in mind: getting the student to put her shoes on and thinking that it was in her best interests to do so.

My dinner companions' suggestions were pretty good, with the exception of my friend Jon's. While he's one of the kindest, fairest, and most generous people I know, his recommendation was to tell her, "Put your fucking shoes on and stop being an asshole." I suggested that this approach would not only make the Barefoot Contessa dig her calloused heels in, but might also prompt an invitation to the dean's office to kiss his shot at tenure good-bye. Momentarily satisfying? Hell, yeah! Productive? No way.

My recommendation was not to make it about the offense of having to look at these dirty, disgusting feet every day, but rather about the social norms this student must learn to follow in order to be successful in the workforce and society in general. Again, play the role of mentor.

> Listen [insert name], I have one goal and one goal only, and that's to prepare you the very best I can for that crazy world that awaits after you leave this place. I want you to be happy and successful and fulfilled. And at some point, that happiness

is going to be predicated on your ability to follow other people's arbitrary rules for how to act, how to dress, et cetera. So consider that part of what I'm teaching you here is the capacity to accept those rules. And you and I both know that no workplace in your future would allow its people to forgo wearing shoes. I would be doing you a disservice if I continued to let you come to class barefoot. If I did, you would be totally unprepared to respond to an employer telling you to wear shoes. So when you come to class tomorrow wearing shoes, think of it a muscle you're developing that will serve you well the rest of your life.

I use this approach often when I am coaching unwilling clients. Sometimes people come to a media training session convinced that they have all the skills they need and that the session will be a paint-by-numbers instruction that insults their intelligence and wastes their time. As I mentioned earlier, this scenario happens a lot with actors and celebrities. After all, they are professional performers who are highly skilled at making people feel something when they perform. They can "turn it on" when the red light on the camera goes on. That's great. It makes my job easy. There's just one problem with that. Their unwavering belief in their own ability usually makes them omit preparation, a fatal mistake for even the most polished performers.

HOW CAN I OUTSHINE MY COLLEAGUES IN MEETINGS?

People hate meetings for a very good reason: They often drag on too long and are so redundant that the only thing left to focus on is the poor etiquette of your colleagues. Bad business behavior in meetings these days is so ubiquitous that anyone who demonstrates exemplary comportment has an excellent chance of being seen as smarter, more confident, and more professional than everyone else.

The good news for you? It's easier to stand out if you don't succumb to any of the following:

The Smartphone Sneak-a-Peak

I'm amazed by how many people routinely commit this basic etiquette mistake. Everyone can tell when you try to secretly check your phone under the table. Don't risk it. In fact, just turn off the phone. That will prevent your phone from distracting others with beeping, buzzing, and ringing.

The Lobotomy Look

Companies often ask me to give junior and midlevel employees a "Meetings 101" seminar. In those sessions, I bring in ten to twelve of them at a time, and I ask them all to go around the table and each give a quick two-minute presentation. Too often, as one person is talking, I'll catch others staring blankly out the window. Just because you don't have the floor doesn't mean you're not being watched. I know you've heard your colleagues' shtick a thousand times, but you need to act as if it's the first time. Look like you're riveted.

Groomed for Failure

Presumably you took care of all necessary grooming before you left the house in the morning, including removing lint from your clothes, peeling dirt from underneath your fingernails, and curling your hair (with a curling iron so you don't do it with your finger during the meeting). I'm not even going to mention noses and ears—too gross. Grooming in front of others is what chimpanzees do, not humans. So *hands off*!

Catering to Yourself

Don't swarm the food tray as if you're just coming off a weeklong cleanse. There is a strict pecking order when it comes to who helps themselves first during a meeting. If you are entertaining clients, then let them lead the way, just as you would never serve yourself dinner before a guest in your home. Similarly, it's a good idea to allow those above you on the corporate ladder to grab food first. If you will be presenting, don't try to multitask with the grub. The last thing you want to do is put your hand over your mouth to give the universal "I'll start talking once I'm done chewing" gesture. Also, the worst time to ask a question is right after a person's taken a bite of food. They will hold you responsible, rightfully so, for putting them in an awkward situation.

The MacBook Airhead Syndrome

This may sound counterintuitive, but don't have your laptop open in front of you during a meeting. Instead of focusing on all the reasons they should be giving you their business, clients may instead be wondering what the heck you're looking at on that screen. Bring a tablet, which when laid flat on the table is an open book to everyone. That way you'll avoid the predicament I witnessed firsthand of a potential client busting an account executive for checking her Facebook page during a meeting. How did she know? The image from the laptop screen reflected off her eyeglasses.

So that takes care of what *not* to do during a meeting. What should you do instead? Follow the Conviction Principle, making sure to use attentive sitting and standing postures. Remember the Curiosity Principle, too. Keep a warm and engaged facial expression while listening intently to what others have to say. Give clients your 100 percent undivided attention.

If you will be presenting, keep your delivery focused on only the content that is relevant to that meeting, and follow the Pasta-Sauce Principle. No one ever complained about a meeting that ran short.

If you are pitching an idea, try to evenly distribute your eye contact around the room. Land on someone, connect with that person and communicate at least part of a thought before moving on to make eye contact with the next. Avoid rapidly pinballing around with your gaze (that looks shifty and nervous), looking off into space (that deprives you of connecting with your listener), or focusing only on the big cheese to the exclusion of his or her support staff. When you come to your big points, *then* zero in on the main decision maker. This ensures that everyone, even the office assistants, are left with a good impression. After the meeting, you can bet that the decision maker asks them, "What did you think of that guy?" You don't want them to exact revenge for being ignored by saying, "I wouldn't trust him."

PITCH-PERFECT POINTER

If you're a baseball fan, you've probably heard of the Alphonse Gaston play. Two players converge on an easy fly ball but at the last minute each backs away expecting the other to catch it. They look at each other as the ball drops between them. This awkward phenomenon can also happen in conference rooms and on conference calls. The last thing you want to do when a client asks a question is for you and your colleague to look at each other and start debating who should handle it. Plan ahead who will handle certain topics and questions. Otherwise that stunned Alphonse Gaston look conveys to the client that neither one of you is particularly keen to take a swing at the question.

On conference calls, it's even more awkward. Two people start talking at once. Then one person says, "You go," but you say, "No, you go," and then there's silence and a lot of time is wasted. If you start talking just ahead of someone else, don't stop. Just keep talking. Eventually the other person will yield and you'll have the floor.

HOW DO I GENTLY ASK SOMEONE TO DITCH THE SMARTPHONE?

Nothing is more annoying than trying to talk to someone who is incessantly checking for e-mails and texts. It's one thing to ask a fellow colleague to ditch the phone. It's quite another to do so when the person holding the phone is a client or someone senior to you in the office.

I faced precisely this predicament not long ago when the head of social media for a large company came to my office for a consult. I was in the middle of a sentence when she picked up her mobile device and checked her text messages.

It put me in an uncomfortable position. Should I ignore what's going on in front of me and just keep talking? No self-respecting professional would do that and risk diminishing his or her stature. But if I addressed it, I could annoy and alienate an important client.

I decided to stop talking and wait, figuring that at some point she would realize that all the sound in the room had stopped. When she put her device down, I continued. It was not unlike training a dog. I had to stop and start a couple more times, but soon she caught on and put the phone away for the rest of the session.

Ironically, on the very day I was writing this chapter, another client, whom I was coaching one-on-one, whipped out his smartphone in the middle of my presentation. I stopped talking but continued writing information on the whiteboard with my back to him. As I was writing, I fully expected to hear over my shoulder, "Sorry about that, I just needed to take care of something." When

I ran out of information to write, I turned around to find him with his face still buried in his iPhone. Remaining calm when confronting one of your major pet peeves is never easy. But after another few seconds of awkward silence, he said, "I finally found that link to the interview I did last November on CNBC if we want to take a look at that together." What a pleasant surprise.

If you doubt whether this digital diversion is legit, you can always try the subtle tactic of saying, "You're way more hi-tech than I am. I could never take notes on my handheld and have them be comprehensible." I have used that line and seen it work to influence the other person into putting down the device.

Another tactic I'll sometimes use is posing a question that shows I'm aware what's going on. "Is there a crisis blowing up back at your office? Let me know if you need a minute or two to handle it, because we can take a break if that would help."

At home it's much easier. I have the iBasket. It's a yellow woven basket that I pass around the dinner table before any food is served. We all deposit our iPhones into it—if we want to eat dinner, that is. I say it's a chance for all of our digital devices to be just like us, to get together and ask how one another's day was.

HOW DO I APOLOGIZE FOR A MISTAKE?

In chapter 1, I told you about my stomach-churning first day at Facebook, when I accidentally went to the wrong building in the wrong town and ended up forty-five minutes late. If my apology had not been Pitch Perfect that day, our thriving business within the tech sector never would have gotten off the ground.

And it would have been easy to do it wrong, as so many people and companies do. Too often, when people apologize, they try to wiggle off the hook and shirk responsibility. If you're going to say "I'm sorry," don't make it halfhearted. An insincere apology is a smarmy way to further alienate yourself from the offended party.

If you are going to fall on your sword, make it one clean thrust. You'll bleed less that way. Don't try to qualify or justify. Don't point fingers or shift the blame. Don't apologize for being late because, "My assistant didn't put it in the calendar." Don't drift into TMI territory, providing endless detailed explanation nobody wants to hear. Many people falsely assume that delving into the minutiae of what went wrong will somehow make everything OK, but this isn't the case. The more details you offer, the worse you look and the more you call the authenticity of your apology into question. My wife has seen and heard it all from students skipping class or not handing in work. This is a typical one:

> Professors,
>
> I am happy to say that as of today I am feeling a good amount better. I can finally breathe partially through my nose, the fever broke, and my energy levels should go up after beginning to eat again. Hopefully I can get more than a couple hours sleep at night and the meds kill the tonsil problem. The health center doesn't offer written excuses, but I signed a document that allows them to speak of me being there if you call.

Perhaps the best approach is to signal to the person receiving the apology that you're happy to give detail, only if it's important for them to hear it. "There were a number of reasons why we failed to deliver, I'm not going to give you the laundry list, but the bottom line is, I'm sorry, I didn't meet your expectations or the ones I set for myself, and here's my plan for getting things back on track."

Think of an apology as a three-part process:

Part 1: Own the mistake. Say something like, "You are absolutely right. That was completely unacceptable and not the outcome I envisioned. I completely understand your disappointment."

Part 2: Couch it as the rare exception—not the norm. I recommend to companies that they apologize concisely and unequivocally. But that doesn't mean that within the apology, you can't allude to what an aberration the mistake is. Even in the apology you are stating that normally you strive for and/or achieve excellence. I didn't do that with Brandee at Facebook, but I could have also said, "You're right: this is a terrible way to start and one that I personally find upsetting because I hold promptness in the highest regard."

Part 3: Forecast a positive result still ahead. In the conversation with Brandee it was vital to pivot to the positive and help her to see ahead to the eventual good result. So while I said, "You are right. There's no worse way to get out of the starting blocks," right on the heels of that was "but I guarantee . . . that once I get there we are going to have an amazing day."

That tactic is so important because no matter what the situation, no matter what the mishap, people essentially want to be reassured by a calming, confident voice that everything's going to be OK.

HOW DO I NAIL A JOB INTERVIEW?

During any given interview, dozens of questions are asked, but only one of them causes nearly all applicants to stumble. See if you can guess which question it is. Is it:

A. What's your greatest weakness?

B. Why should we hire you?

C. If you were a tree, what kind of tree would you be? (aka the Barbara Walters job-interview question)

D. Tell me about yourself.

Do you have your answer ready?

The right answer is the one that seems the easiest to answer. It's also the one that seems the least important and the most casual: Tell me about yourself. Lucy Cherkasets, our executive director at Clarity Media Group, once worked as director of human resources of a prestigious New York PR firm, and the answers she heard to "Tell me about yourself" will probably floor you:

"I'm fine."

"I'm feeling good today."

"My name is Suzanne, and I was born in 1970, and I grew up in Montana. My parents were really religious and . . ."

"I was born in New York and I'm generally from Brooklyn. On my résumé, it says I am in Dallas but I really live in New York. . . ."

"Well, you would not believe the kind of weekend I had! I went to the shore with my boyfriend and we got stuck in this three-hour traffic jam. He and I got in a fight about the traffic and by the time we got to the shore we were broke up. Worst. Weekend. Ever!"

Why do so many people destroy their chances on such a seemingly easy question? Because "Tell me about yourself" is deceptive. It doesn't sound like a trick question, or even a thought-provoking one, so many people skip over it when preparing for an interview. Instead, they spend their time on seemingly tougher questions like, "What's your biggest weakness?"

In reality, it's the toughest question of the entire interview and also the most important one to get right. That's because it's often the very first question, so the Headline Principle applies. Get it right and you've increased your chances of being in the running for the job. Get it wrong and the interviewer starts thinking, "Next!"

"These are really educated people," Lucy explains, "but they end up telling the interviewer a bunch of nothing when they answer that question. The interviewer doesn't want a timeline. The interviewer doesn't want to know where you've been the past ten years. The interviewer wants to know why they are at the table. And if they bomb that first question, they've lost the interviewer's attention completely."

That's why Lucy helps clients prepare their answers to this question more than any other. In one case, she and a client spent three hours preparing a response. If that amount of prep sounds absurd to you, you're probably not preparing for your job interviews properly.

To prepare your answer to this and other questions, lean on the Scorsese Principle. Think in stories and visual analogies and details. Before the interview, come up with three to five stories that illustrate your strengths and points you'd like to make, and think of how you might be able to use those stories to answer typical interview questions. But don't think of the interview as a Q&A session. Think of it as a presentation.

"When the interviewer goes back to her team to talk about the twenty different candidates she's seen that day, it's the stories that will stick out in her mind," Lucy says. "She might not remember Sally from Susan, but, if you give her memorable stories, she will remember you."

The other place that many people stumble is at the end, when the interviewer asks, "So, do you have any questions for me?"

If you've made it this far, that means the interviewer sees your potential. Don't change her mind by asking her a question that she's already answered during the interview.

"Don't marry your questions," Lucy says. If the interviewer happened to answer all your questions, say so. Don't waste the interviewer's time by asking questions just for the sake of asking questions. Just say, "I'm looking forward to the next steps," thank the interviewer, and shake hands.

HOW DO I ASK FOR A PROMOTION OR RAISE?

Women seem to have a particularly tough time when it comes to asking for raises and promotions. A University of Chicago study found that, in response to an explicit salary offer, only 8 percent of women tried to negotiate for more pay. That's compared to 11 percent of men. Other research finds that men are nine times more likely than women to ask for more money when searching for jobs.

I'd like to do everything possible to reverse this trend and help everyone earn what they are worth. Whether you are a woman or a man, I hope the following advice helps you accomplish that goal.

Don't Make It About What Anyone Owes You

Don't go in with hat in hand, saying, "I've been here for two years, and everyone else has gotten raises except me." Remember, your boss thinks of the workplace as a meritocracy, not an entitlement program. That's the surest way to be seen as a cost, instead of an asset.

Give Your Boss a Bargain

Take a tip from what companies do when they want you to pay more for something. Companies don't just increase the rate or price, they offer more services so they can charge the customer more. You want to convey to your boss, "You are tapping into only a fraction of how incredibly valuable I can be to you." Another effective tactic is to show you've been thinking about one of the company's areas of need and devising strategies to improve it. "I've been spending a lot of time analyzing the way we go about doing. . . . And I've come up with some plans I know you'll like. If you're willing to let me take a shot at this, I'm ready to tackle it. The salary adjustment I would be looking for to do it, because it is more responsibility, would be far outweighed by the benefits we would see."

Know the Bargain Before You Walk In

While you are sitting in front of your boss is not the time to come up with evidence of your value. You want to know how you will convey this long before you walk in the door. Have specific ideas ready, ideas that address real needs your boss has. You want to be able to say, "This is where you have needs, and this is how I can respond to them for you."

Be Specific

Show precisely how you will either help save or make the company money. Then reveal the bargain, "What I would be asking for salarywise would be just a fraction of that."

HOW DO I ASK FOR A FAVOR WITHOUT FEELING INDEBTED?

One thing I learned early from my parents: no one wants to be asked for a favor they can't make happen. It exposes their limitations and reminds them that they don't have the power or the clout to help. So ask at your own risk. If they can't deliver, you may end up harming a key relationship.

Picking the right person to ask may not come down solely to an accurate assessment of this person's clout. Perhaps she has the power to help, but not the time. Or maybe he has the time and the clout, but someone closer to him beat you to the punch and has already asked him for the same favor.

Getting around this is simple: don't ask for favors. Instead, ask for advice. Everyone has advice. When you ask for it, no one feels exposed or limited. To the contrary, seeking advice makes most people feel wise, important, and needed. It's just plain flattering.

Think of the difference between "Do you have a moment? I'd like to ask for a favor" and "Do you have a moment? I'd like to get your take on something."

The first is almost an automatic turndown, isn't it? If someone asked you that question, your first response might be, "Well, now isn't a good time."

But the second most likely gets you inside the office. Keep in mind that this is not a trick. You're not telling someone that you want to ask for advice but then, in reality, hitting them up for a favor. No, you really *are* asking for advice. That's because the people who would say yes if you asked them for advice will probably volunteer to help you if they are so inclined. You don't even need to ask. Whereas the people who would say no would never offer to help you anyway.

In this way, you can vet people without putting them in the awkward position of having to turn you down.

HOW DO I CONGRATULATE A COLLEAGUE ON A PROMOTION THAT I WANTED FOR MYSELF?

Congratulations are usually pretty simple when we're genuinely happy about someone's promotion. But when the kiss-ass who isn't half as talented as you gets rewarded, that's when your graciousness and acting ability get put to the ultimate test.

You don't want to be in a position of saying "I'm so happy for you" when you're not. And if it's the office creep, you certainly don't want to force the lie "I wish you a lot of luck." It's fake and it will sound so. The only luck you're wishing this person is bad luck so they mess up, get fired, and make way for the rightful occupant of that job: you!

A certain degree of honesty is key, but you want to strike a balance between honesty and grace. And you want to keep it short.

The Pasta-Sauce Principle is the way to go. The more you talk, the more apparent it will be that you are not happy.

The best way to congratulate a colleague depends, in large part, on how you feel about the colleague.

- If it's someone you respect, say, "If it wasn't going to be me, I couldn't be happier that it's you."
- If it's the office backstabber and you're sick to your stomach that this person has leapfrogged over you, say, "Congrats. I hope the post is everything you are expecting it to be." As much as it galls you, that keeps you from having to be overtly dishonest.

WHAT'S THE SECRET TO BEING A GRACEFUL MODERATOR?

Great moderators are not born. They are practiced, and they do their homework. They don't wait until the day of the presentation to come up with their questions. They research and preinterview each guest. By presentation day, they already have a good idea of what each panelist is likely to say, along with the questions most likely to bring out those responses. Use this advice:

- Plan and structure the panel based on how much time you have, the number of topics to be discussed, and the number of participants. If the panel is scheduled to last one hour, and you have four topic areas to be discussed, then obviously you have approximately fifteen minutes per topic (more like fourteen if you factor in your introduction and wrap-up at the end). If you have four participants, then you must keep each of them to under three and a half minutes (you have to allow for your questions and conversational involvement). If you put your questions on a PowerPoint or Keynote on your tablet, you can configure the preview screen to show you a countdown clock. That will help keep the program moving according to schedule.

- Use the Pasta-Sauce Principle, especially in your introductory remarks. In the briefest time possible, your intro should outline the issue to be discussed, articulate why it's vital enough to warrant a panel discussion, and forecast how the conclusions of the panel may in some way be constructive.

- Don't be reluctant to start with a provocative question that gets the discussion off to a rousing start. Starting the discussion with some type of "lightning round," in which each panel member gets thirty seconds to respond to the first question, can be a good way not to let everyone get cold while the first person hogs the floor.

- Mix up the length of your questions. It's fine to ask a longer, thoughtful question, but also blend in shorter, punchier questions to create a more stimulating pace, especially on follow-ups.

- Avoid asking multipronged questions. Save the "and if so" part of the question for a follow-up.

- Don't telegraph your question by stating at the beginning of the question whom it's intended for. Save that for the very end. The idea is to keep the panelists slightly off balance in order to capture the most spontaneous, least-rehearsed answers. The more time they have to prepare for a question they know is theirs, the better they can avoid answering a direct question and go to their predetermined message points. Keeping the guests away from canned responses is the best way to generate some news out of the event.

- Don't prove how much you know in the question. A long factual setup to a question tends to be boring and slows down the pacing of the event. If you need to provide context to the question, do it in a concise bullet-point format.

- Be aware of your panelists' positions on the designated issue and then juxtapose conflicting viewpoints. If two of your panelists put forth position A and two adhere to position B, then call on them in an A B A B sequence.

- Avoid asking each panelist to weigh in on the same question. As you segue from one guest to another, advance the topic of the discussion slightly so the event feels as though it's moving forward.

- If two panelists square off, let them go without your involvement until the debate starts sounding repetitive. If the friction starts to subside, your job as moderator is to subtly "fan the flames," as we used to say in the control room at CBS when Charlie Rose had guests who were poised to start duking it out.

- Don't be so obsessed with your next question that you stop listening to the conversation around you. If one of your panelists said something controversial or newsworthy and you were looking down at your list of questions and missed it, that would be a disaster.

- Be prepared to shine a spotlight on something fascinating that a panelist downplays or glosses over. For instance, if your guest said, "Our company grew at a brisk pace for over a decade, and that growth positioned us to be an attractive acquisition. In fact, at one point we turned down a one-billion-dollar offer, but now we're managing a more modest growth period."

  You would need to be the one to jump in and say, "Whoa! Wait a minute! You said no to a billion-dollar buyout? What was your thinking behind that?" Don't let the content your audience might be most interested in just wash away.

- Save a thought-provoking, forward-thinking question for last. It can be one that calls on panelists to be reflective in the hopes someone will say something poignant. You can also ask them to predict how things will change in a few years with regard to your topic.

IN MODERATING A PANEL, HOW DO I GENTLY CUT OFF PEOPLE WHO TALK TOO MUCH?

I often coach people who moderate, and frequently they pose this question. It seems no matter how much you coach panelists to stay within their allotted time, someone inevitably talks far longer, ignoring all your subtle hand signals to wrap things up.

When this happens, you can feel the energy in the room sag. It also takes the edge off the other panelists. It's your job as moderator to keep all participants involved. Don't allow the blowhards to dominate. It is up to you to draw the less-vocal guests into the mix.

Before I get into how to cut people off, let's play a little offense. You can prevent most people from dominating the floor with some preparation ahead of time.

Draw up an outline of the topics you want the panel to address and the order you want the panel to address them. From there, do some math. Based on how much time you have for your panel, divvy up how long you want to stay on each topic and how long you want each panelist to speak. Then preinterview each panelist. This will give you a sense ahead of time how each will respond to your questions, and how long each is likely to talk. This is a great opportunity to coach panelists not only on time, but also on delivery. For instance, you can suggest that panelists tell visual stories to make their points.

Based on your interviews, you can then refine your questions and develop follow-up questions that allow you to draw out the anecdotes you like from each participant and direct conversational traffic to the next panelist.

Arriving with that information will be immensely helpful, especially if one of your panelists tries to turn the event into a long-winded monologue. Preventing that requires a delicate balance between being too meek and losing control of the discussion, and stifling the feel of a free-flow conversation by being too rigid and heavy-handed. To deftly apply the brakes to your runaway panelist, avoid the clumsy options like, "I'm going to have to leave it there" or "You've gone overtime. Sorry, I have to get some of the other guests in." You shouldn't need to be a traffic cop. You should be an organic part of the conversation.

Instead, use the Camouflaged Cutoff from chapter 9. Look for an opportunity to finish one of the Egg-Timer Narcissist's sentences. Don't think of yourself as being rude. Rather think of it as taking the baton in a relay race.

Chances are, you'll soon find a moment when you can guess how your panelist is going to finish a thought. So wedge yourself in, finish the sentence, and even talk over your panelist if you have to. Whatever you do, don't stop talking. Once you know you have the floor, quickly yet subtly transition to a new topic or ask one of the other panelists for their thoughts on what they just heard. For instance, you might say:

"Something you just said triggered another thought just now, and it has to do with a related topic. . . ."

"What's interesting about your take on this is that it's the polar-opposite position to Karen's. Karen, what do you think about this?"

"I'm curious what the rest of you think about this, because I know you feel very strongly about this issue."

I'M ON A PANEL. HOW DO I MAKE THE BEST IMPRESSION?

Many people show up for their panel hoping that they'll somehow be able to give an A-plus answer to every question the moderator or audience tosses their way.

Just because a panel discussion is a more casual setting, that does not lessen the importance of thorough preparation.

Before your panel discussion, ask yourself, "What is most interesting to the average audience member? Where's the value in what I have to say? Am I offering a unique perspective? Am I providing some guidance or wisdom on something that will help them in their day-to-day life?" It's far easier to prepare your content for a panel than a media interview for one simple reason: Moderators share their questions in advance, whereas a journalist rarely does. Once you know the questions in advance, preparing your content is like batting practice. You know exactly what's being thrown and where, so you can put your best swing on it.

As you prepare your content, remember the Scorsese Principle: be a storyteller. Road-test your stories out loud on family or friends. That way you can tell if they're too long or whether they're boring even to you.

During the actual panel, use this additional advice.

Ignore Emily Post

Don't ask for permission to speak and don't sit on your hands and wait to be called on. The audience wants to feel as though they're watching you shoot the breeze over a beer or a cup of coffee. They don't want to watch a rigid, formal process. It's better to wedge yourself in and keep your content tight than to sit back and wait your turn.

Embrace the notion that not all conversational traffic has to flow through the moderator. You can say to another panelist, "It's so interesting you say that, because we're dealing with something so similar on our front," and steer the conversation where you want it to go.

Detour as Needed

If the specific question is so weird that you don't want to touch it, the Draper Principle comes into play. Address the topic of the question rather than the question itself. For instance, say you work for the post office and someone asks you, "So is there any truth to the belief that people who work for the post office are more mentally unstable than people who work for other government offices? The expression 'going postal,' for instance—is there any validity to it?" That is not a question you want to answer, so don't stay in the toxicity zone. Broaden it into an issue about how perceptions can be distorted. Your answer might be: "It's interesting, because we just did a survey last quarter. We asked all postal worker about their satisfaction level on the job and compared it to other agencies, and we ranked third out of twenty. I'd have to say from my own experience that people like their jobs at the post office. Like any other job, there will be stress at times, but all in all, it's a great place to work."

Keep Your Curious Face on at All Times

Often panelists come to life only when they have the floor. That's a shortsighted strategy that can backfire and reflect poorly on you. The audience can still see you, even if your mouth isn't moving. Don't look bored while others are talking or, worse, sport that bitchy resting face that I mentioned in chapter 8.

This issue frequently comes up when I work with the entire executive leadership team of a public company to prep for their annual shareholders meeting. The focus of the training session is technically about each of them standing and presenting while the rest of the team sits behind them on the stage. Inevitably, I end up reminding almost all of them that even though it's not their turn at the podium, they're still *on*. Most have detached, bored looks on their faces, not a good idea, given that they're visible to the audience.

Try not to appear as though you're daydreaming and merely waiting for your turn to speak. You should feel tired after these events from all that time being on. When the other panelists are talking, sit forward, look interested, and be ready to jump in.

HOW DO I INTRODUCE A FAMOUS GUEST?

It always drives me nuts when I attend a panel featuring someone famous, only to have the moderator deliver the dreaded cliché: "My next guest needs no introduction." And then what do they do? They proceed to not just read an intro, but recite that person's entire CV. Please regard this short passage as the official memo I'm circulating: *Don't do that!*

Recently I had the pleasure of coaching a Wall Street client who was asked to do a panel-style, one-on-one interview at a conference with former secretary of state Hillary Clinton. Now there's a woman who needs no intro, but of course I helped craft one, concise and worthy of her stature. He started out with a bold statement that underscored her distinctiveness:

> Never in the history of our government has one person carried so much influence and devoted so much energy to public service in so many vital roles over such an impressive stretch of time as my next guest. Whether it was as secretary of state, United States senator, or First Lady, Hillary Clinton has reminded us what a powerful combination a keen intellect can be when paired with an indefatigable drive to make the world a better place.

Then a succinct checklist of specific accomplishments:

> She restored civility to our foreign-policy efforts, building stronger relationships with Europe and establishing new relationships in Asia.
>
> She responded directly and swiftly to the complex challenges in Iran and North Korea and elsewhere in the world.
>
> She was a strong supporter of free enterprise around the world, furthering US business interests overseas and creating jobs in a challenging economic environment.

And she was an unwaveringly strong voice in support of all human rights.

Then putting the guest's gravitas in some grander historical perspective:

When we all look back at the Clinton era in the Senate and State Department, this will be known as a time when America's standing in the world was restored and our foreign policy was recalibrated in effectively dealing with the most pressing issues of the world.

Now the final tease of how engaging this opportunity to hear her speak will be:

I am certain all of her insights and wisdom are of tremendous interest to us all and we are all excited about what she is about to share with us today.

There wasn't much else that followed. Piling on layer after layer of obsequious accolades would just end up sounding sycophantic. Nobody likes that.

HOW DO I GET RID OF THE PRESPEECH JITTERS?

I want this book to accomplish for all who read it what the vibe in the Clarity Media Group office achieves for the clients who visit us: instill a sense of calm, confidence, and relaxation. Giving you strategies on how to get rid of the anxiety you feel in the pit of your stomach in the days, hours, and moments before giving a speech or presentation can go a long way toward realizing that goal.

Everyone feels some anxiety before speaking. If you felt none, there'd be something wrong. I've given countless speeches over the years, and I still feel a little jumpy before all of them.

Some presentations bring on more anxiety than others. Recently I was asked to speak to a group of executives of a major company on how to improve their executive presence and public-speaking skills. The event planners urged me to come early so I could watch the speaker slotted right before me. "He's an ah-*maaay*-zing speaker," they gushed, "fantastic, superengaging!"

So of course my first thought was, *Great. Just what I need—some show-off setting the bar excruciatingly high for me. Do I really want to subject myself to this?* But naturally I was curious to find out what their definition of ah-*maaay*-zing was. I wanted to know if I was the synonym or antonym. The downside of satisfying my curiosity was that if he was really good, I would end up psyching myself out, trying too hard and wandering out of my performance sweet spot. So I elected to stay outside the auditorium and follow my own advice of knowing the first two to three minutes of the presentation *cold*. So I said it multiple times in a low whisper until I knew it backward and forward.

After I tackled everything on my own prepresentation checklist, I let my curiosity get the better of me, and I walked into the auditorium to see what size oratory shoes I would be trying to fill. My biggest fear was encountering a Tony Robbins type up there with the audience in the palm of his hand. Imagine my relief and delight when I discovered somebody possessing all the storytelling savvy of Alan Greenspan. What a relief that the event planners' definition of ah-*maaay*-zing was closer to my definition of mediocre. Bye-bye stomach butterflies!

The prespeech jitters are common, and they are probably what I get asked about the most. To calm your nerves, follow this advice.

Practice the Beginning Over and Over Again

The first two minutes of any presentation are when you're most nervous. A strong, smooth opening is like a perfect triple axel at the start of an Olympic figure skater's routine. Nailing it is a confidence builder and helps get rid of the butterflies.

Skip the Extra Cup of Coffee

It can make you feel jumpy and jittery. On those rare occasions when you're feeling sluggish right before you're on, eat a piece of fruit. It's the quickest way to raise your blood sugar level for an energy spike.

Sneak in a Workout

A morning workout can make you feel relaxed and confident. If it's part of your daily routine, don't skip it just because you're getting up early. Aerobics also helps you expel some built-up physical energy that anxiety can cause.

Get to a Venue ahead of Time

Get up on stage before the audience files in so you can get the feel of the room. Stand at the lectern or onstage. Sit in the chairs. Talk through the microphone and hear the sound of your voice. Once that's done, head straight for the room where everyone is mingling around the coffee urns and croissants. If possible, work the room and the guests and try to get to know some of them. I never skip this opportunity, because a series of brief conversations with the people who will be in your audience is a great way to relax. Seizing on the opportunity to socialize beforehand means that, during my presentation, I will be looking out into a sea of somewhat familiar faces rather than total strangers. And those audience members with whom I've chatted will feel more invested in being engaged listeners, often flashing a warmer look of recognition on their faces. When I have conversations in advance, I also frequently hear interesting observations or anecdotes that I can seamlessly incorporate into my presentation to give it a spontaneous feel.

Warm Up Before You Begin

Say aloud what you plan to say, whether it's in the taxi on the way to the event or in a private room away from the gathering. This not only calms nerves, it also prevents you from getting off to a slow start.

Think Success

Project in your mind that the audience will be enthralled. The last thing you want is to have a sudden wave of self-doubt right before you have to be great. Don't question whether your presentation will fly or allow doubt to creep into your thoughts. Don't wonder if it's good enough or if it will interest the audience. Instead, think of times you've delivered the material in the past and how much the audience loved it.

Walk to the Lectern. Take a Breath. Then Talk.

Many clients ask me, "How do I get rid of that shake and tremble in my voice? It's a dead giveaway that I'm petrified." That condition is caused by something as simple as breathing. When we're anxious and panicked, we forget to breathe properly. We take short, shallow breaths that raise the heart rate (that's why it feels like it's about to pound out of your chest) and deplete our lungs of the air we need to project the voice.

One other possibility: physical exertion, even something as minor as running up a short flight of stairs on the way to the lectern. The problem is, even if you're just slightly winded, once you start talking, you can't fully catch your breath.

In 1981, as President Ronald Reagan was in the hospital following John Hinckley's assassination attempt, Secretary of State Alexander Haig was in the Situation Room at the White House. He watched a monitor showing Deputy Press Secretary Larry Speakes in the pressroom answering questions. Leslie Stahl asked, "Who is running the government?" Speakes stumbled, admitting he could not answer the question at that time.

Haig ran from the Situation Room to the pressroom and announced, "I am in control here."

His arms were shaking and his knees were wobbling. His voice sounded pinched. He seemed anything but in control.

Was it nerves? Was he shaken? Or had he not stopped briefly to catch his breath after running to the pressroom? We'll never know for sure, but I'm betting it was the latter.

It's easy to get out of breath. I once listened to a talk given by the news president of one of the major broadcast networks. This man is a solid speaker, but he wasn't where he needed to be before this particular talk. For some reason he was downstairs on a lower level instead of just offstage when he was introduced. He ran up a flight of stairs so as not to be late to the microphone. When he walked onstage, he was winded, and he stayed that way through virtually the entire speech.

Breathe Deeply Just before and during Your Talk

Take long inhales through your nose, hold them for a beat or two, and then exhale long and slowly through your mouth. If you do yoga, you know how to do this already. This calms you down, slows your pulse, and replenishes your lungs, restoring a stable and confident sound to your voice.

Slow Down

The No-Tailgating Principle is especially important during the first ninety seconds of any talk. During that all-important minute and a half, you must concentrate on having a controlled pace, because everything in your body is going to tell you to hit the gas and go very, very fast. It's also important whenever you hit a rocky stretch. Often when people make a mistake, they feel as though they've lost pacing and need to make up the time. Accelerating your pace in the wake of a mistake only increases the likelihood that you will make additional errors.

Look at the Right Faces

If you're presenting in front of a group of people, chances are you'll find more than your fair share of BRFs (bitchy resting faces) in the audience. Don't follow the cliché advice of imagining those people in their underwear. Instead, think of them as a solar eclipse that'll blind you if you dare look in their direction. Rather, find the BFFs, the best-friend faces I mentioned in chapter 8. They're the ones who smile adoringly and nod like bobble-head dolls. There's a good likelihood that in a crowd of ten or more, you'll be able to find a couple of BFFs. If you're speaking to a bigger audience, see if you can spot one BFF in each quadrant of the room—near left, far left, near right, far right—and play to just those four people. They will boost your confidence immeasurably. If somehow your eyes inadvertently catch people on their smartphones, don't automatically assume that they're texting with someone. Psyche yourself into thinking that they are furiously attempting to chronicle as much of the wisdom pouring out of your mouth as their little thumbs can take down.

You see a pattern developing here? Always presume the best, not the worst. If the eyelids of someone in my audience start to get very heavy, I tell myself that they must have partied very late the previous night. And when my eyes accidentally lock with those of that solar-eclipse audience member, I remind myself that their off-in-the-ozones facial expression is just their default listening expression even when they're captivated.

HOW DO I TAKE A SIP OF WATER DURING A SPEECH?

It's probably better that you take this advice from me and not Marco Rubio, who will forever be known as the senator from Florida who tried to sneak a sip of water during a live nationally televised speech. If you have never seen the clip, watch it. You will learn why it's ridiculous to try to sneak a sip of water, when doing so unapologetically looks so much more confident.

It sounds so basic, but always hydrate before you orate. Diction and enunciation improve measurably when your mouth is moist. I'm reminded of this every month when I narrate news stories for *Consumer Reports.* The producers plop down fifteen scripts in front of me to voice-over. When I start slurring a word here and there or stumbling on a group of words that are hard to pronounce, I stop and take a drink of water, and magically the delivery is much clearer and mistake-free. Water is an elixir for your mouth when you need it to be spot-on with pronunciation.

Being well hydrated also allows you to avoid two of the most dreaded afflictions to curse any public speaker. One is that little elastic string of mucus that diabolically attaches itself to both your upper and lower lip and just refuses to go away. And like lipstick on a woman's front teeth, often the speaker is humiliatingly unaware of this. Sure, it's gross, but worse, the audience has long ceased absorbing the speaker's message. Secretly they're both repulsed and fascinated by how long that bugger can stretch up and down like Silly Putty before breaking.

Then there are those white half circles that form at the corners of your mouth, the kind you see on someone who's been discovered wandering the desert for days without water. For these reasons, a bottle of water can spare you unwanted embarrassment.

I lived to regret the one time I forgot to come to a speaking engagement with water. I had agreed to address a graduate class at NYU on dealing with the media. About ten minutes into my talk, it felt as though a tiny feather had flown down my windpipe. I toyed briefly with the idea of running out of the room and finding the nearest water fountain but thought that might not be appropriate for someone claiming to be an accomplished public speaker. The only water nearby was the bottle that the professor had been drinking from. At that moment, the choice was simple: endure a little backwash or have the Heimlich maneuver performed on me. He kindly offered me his Poland Spring, and I understood his preference to toss it after I took a couple of lifesaving sips.

Whether you're walking into a meeting, a job interview, a presentation, or a webcast interview, *always* bring water, and take a sip right before you begin. Any break in the action, a video clip in your presentation, or someone asking a question during your remarks, is a perfect opportunity to wet your whistle again. In fact, you can even take a needed drink if you're speaking without interruption. But there's a right way and wrong way to do it. The *wrong* way is to stop your speaking too early and create ten to fifteen seconds of dead air while you:

1. Walk over to the bottle
2. Unscrew the cap
3. Lift the bottle to your lips
4. Take a big sip
5. Swallow
6. Screw the cap back on
7. Place it back down

The *right* way to take an unobtrusive swig is to keep talking through all the above stages, except obviously during numbers 4 and 5. Doing it the right way may only cause a two- or three-second delay, which is no big deal. If you have a funny line coming up that generates a laugh, that's also a good opportunity to take a drink. Better to do it prophylactically during one of these short breaks before you really need to do it.

HOW DO I REMEMBER WHAT I WANT TO SAY DURING A PRESENTATION?

Many clients tell me, "I just want to get through this thing." They don't want a single thing to go wrong. They plan their talks too much, and they expect that everything will go exactly to plan. They don't want a single word out of place.

As a result, they flatten out and deliver what is perhaps a technically sound yet forgettable speech. I would rather you not focus on eliminating all mistakes and instead put your back into it and demonstrate the value of what you are delivering. My definition of perfect is not mistake-free. To me, perfection in communication is being real, casual, warm, and enthusiastic.

Part of coming across authentic means that you shouldn't read your speech from a script. Don't try to sit down at a computer and write out your presentation, unless you've written for television and know how to write for the ear. When you are typing, you are writing for the eye. Instead, try these three steps:

1. Make a thorough outline of your presentation on 5×8 note cards.
2. Get up and talk through your presentation from just the outline while rolling audio or video from your smartphone or tablet.
3. Transcribe the audio you've recorded.

This now becomes the text of your presentation instead of something you sat down at your computer to write. This is merely a verbatim safety net. It is still not something you're ever going to memorize or read from, but only text to help keep you consistent when you rehearse. It will be much more conversational and personal, and you will avoid the formality that makes some people sound stilted.

Putting your content on note cards is key. Don't make the mistake of printing out your text on pieces of paper, and whatever you do, don't staple or paper clip them together. If you do, flipping from page to page will be a noisy, conspicuous, and clumsy undertaking. Plus, if you're nervous and your hands are slightly shaking, holding sheets of paper will just make your anxiety obvious to your audience.

I witnessed this recently when a client introduced me to a group of executives I was about to train. She was reading from my printed-out bio, and the piece of paper she was holding was flapping all around and making a racket. Had she not been holding a sheet of paper, I probably never would have noticed that her hands were shaking.

In contrast, 5×8 index cards are stiff, eliminating all of these drawbacks. Plus, for men, they fit inside the inner breast pocket of a jacket. They also anchor your hands in a proper resting position if you hold them against your torso instead of out in front of you and away from your body. They're also small enough that you can still use your hands to gesticulate even though you're holding them.

If you need to look at the cards to remind yourself what you're saying next, move the cards away from your body, briefly glance down, then look up and return the cards (and your hands) to their resting position. One more tip? Because your cards are not going to be attached, number them in the lower right corner. This is what I call butterfingers insurance. If in your haste you dropped your cards right before getting up to speak, you otherwise might put them back in the wrong order. I have seen that happen. It's not a pretty sight when a speaker flips from card 2 straight to card 4 and realizes he's skipped a whole section only after a couple of sentences are already out of his mouth.

If you are called upon to make a formal speech rather than a presentation, then you will likely have full text in front of you on the lectern. Here, working from heavier stock stationery is best for two reasons:

1. Heavier stock is quieter to handle than flimsy typing paper.
2. Because it's thicker, it's easier to separate the sheets with your thumb and forefinger when you turn the page, reducing the possibility of accidentally sliding two pages to the side at once.

Again, no staples, no paper clips. And for good measure, put your ordered sheets inside a clear plastic or manila folder. Then when you get to the lectern, slide the pages out of the folder and create two piles: the pile you're reading from and one just to the side onto which you will slide the pages you've completed. It's not a flipping over; it's a slide, which is quieter and less conspicuous. I also don't like speeches put into a three-ring, school-style, loose-leaf binder. In that situation, you have no choice but to flip the finished pages over, just an overt reminder to your audience that, yes, you are reading instead of talking.

On your printed speech, use a yellow highlighter to mark your key moments, the content that is meant to resonate deepest with your audience. This will serve as a visual reminder to lift your head and make solid and meaningful eye contact with the audience. If you are looking down and reading during your key points, the impact will be lost. But of course we all feel anxiety when our eyes leave the page. It's driven by the fear that when you look back down to resume, your eyes will encounter a cluttered sea of words and you won't be able to quickly find your place. To alleviate that fear, increase the font size of your pickup point so you can find it easily.

If you want to go high tech, you can experiment with putting your speech on your iPad. There's a terrific app called Teleprompt+ that mimics a professional teleprompter by scrolling your copy at whatever speed you choose. If it's moving too fast or too slow at any point, a simple finger drag on the screen can compensate. I have some executive clients who have taken to this method quickly and easily and now would never dream of going back to a printout.

PITCH-PERFECT POINTER

Just as you would never build a house or a car without specific design plans, you should never venture into speaking on the record without your own detailed blueprint of what you'll say. The best communicators make it look spontaneous, but it isn't. That said, don't overrehearse what you plan to say. It can come out sounding recited and wooden. The more you become wedded to verbatim, scripted responses, the more detached you grow from your own words. Leave a little bit of room for spontaneity.

HOW DO I KEEP AN AUDIENCE FROM FALLING ASLEEP?

Buckle your seat belt: here comes another automotive analogy. You know how easy it is to fall asleep in the back of a car that's humming down the highway on cruise control? Speaking in a monotonous, unchanging pace is the public-speaking equivalent. It's like putting your audience in an infant car seat and taking them for a smooth ride close to bedtime. It's one of the surest ways to induce slumber. Conversely, I don't think I've ever managed to fall asleep in a New York City taxicab navigating through rush-hour stop-and-go traffic. So to keep your audience alert, include pauses, change the pitch and pace of your voice, mix the theoretical with the specific, alter the structure of your sentences, and vary the volume of your voice. Variance is the key. Keep mixing it up and don't fall into predictable patterns.

When you alter your pace, go briskly through the conversational parts of the text, the information that's secondary in importance, and then slow down when you get to the key messages. Use a slower, more deliberate pace for the information you want to resonate most deeply. Draw the words out as if you are elongating their pronunciation. If you maintain the same voice modulation throughout, the audience has a hard time discerning what's really important.

However, if you raise the volume of your voice every time you get to a key message, that technique becomes predictable and loses effectiveness in stimulating the audience's ear. Sometimes, when you get to a key message, pull back and lower your voice while keeping the intensity in the delivery. Then when you begin the next thought, bring your voice back full. You are trying to bring the audience along on an unpredictable joyride on which they're not at all sure what's going to happen next.

You can also:

- Craft your primary messages like the punch lines of a joke, in which you build to them with a little sense of drama. Deliver them like a punch line as well—slow your pacing and then let a beat of pause follow before you deliver the point.
- Provide some advance warning that you're about to deliver an important point. Lines like, "More than anything else right now, the biggest factor driving the sales is this: . . ." These drumroll lines allow you to build to a crescendo.
- Maintain good, meaningful eye contact with your audience, especially during your key points. When you look in one direction or at one person, commit to that line of sight for two or three beats, and then look in another direction or at another person. Anything faster will make you look nervous and shifty.

THE TOP SEVEN WAYS SPEAKERS
BLOW THEIR PRESENTATIONS

1. Open their talk by saying, "I'd like to start off this morning by first spending a little time discussing . . ." There's no need to spend valuable time announcing what you're about to do. Just do it. Don't get bogged down in agenda setting. Instead, dive right into your subject matter.
2. Announce that they're about to tell a story or make an analogy.
3. Gesticulate in a predictable, rhythmic way, making the same hand gesture every five seconds. This is distracting.
4. Deliver every word at the same speed, as if they're on cruise control.
5. Forget they are wearing a microphone that picks up the sounds of everything they do, including blowing their nose or clearing their throat. To avoid the need to clear your throat, drink plenty of water and avoid dairy, which creates mucus.
6. Wear long earrings. Not only are they distracting, they can also clang against headsets and microphones.
7. Ask people afterward, "How did I do?" No one ever tells you the truth. Even if you were mediocre, most people respond, "You were great." If you sincerely want to improve, ask people, "Give me two things I should change when I do this presentation next time." This swings the door wide open for constructive criticism.

PITCH-PERFECT POINTER

Just the word *PowerPoint* makes many people groan, and for good reason. Too many people abuse the software, and we've all had at least one (or perhaps hundreds) of experiences of sitting through boring presentations that went on far too long. If you are planning to use PowerPoint, follow these golden rules:

- Limit yourself to twelve slides.
- Put no more than four bullets on each slide.
- Use no more than five or six words in each bullet.
- See if it's possible to have just imagery on the slides—no words.
- Never read the text on your slide.
- Do not hand out a printed copy of the deck in advance.

If you distribute the deck in advance, all you're going to see is the tops of people's heads, because they will be looking down at the pages, not up at you. And chances are, they will be jumping ahead to the final page while you're somewhere in the middle. This creates a total disconnection and disengagement. Instead, offer to e-mail the deck following your presentation.

Think of you and your PowerPoint as two announcers in a broadcast booth for a sporting event. Your deck is the play-by-play announcer. You are the color commentator. You are intended to provide complementary, not redundant, information.

HOW CAN I GIVE BETTER INTERVIEWS?

This book simply wouldn't be complete if I didn't give you at least some advice about how to handle yourself when being interviewed by the media. After all, I've spent time in both positions, as the interviewer and the interviewee. I've also trained countless people on how to excel in both situations.

Perhaps the most important point I can convey to you is this: never lose sight of the fact that you agreed to do this interview because there is something specific you need to get out of the experience. You did not agree to this interview because you enjoy doing a favor for the journalist. You didn't do it because you want to be famous. You agreed because you have information you wish to share, and the journalist is serving as your bullhorn. Chances are, you're seizing this opportunity in order to promote your brand or organization. Whatever your reasons, your motivation should be the filter through which your every thought and word passes. This is one of those situations in life when it's OK to have entirely selfish motivations.

Before the interview, identify two or three key messages and make a commitment to say them even if the interviewer doesn't ask you questions that perfectly tee those messages up. It is up to you to independently drive to your key messages if necessary. Be determined to say them. If you don't, consider your interview a wasted opportunity. Identify anecdotes you can tell that illustrate each message. In addition, prepare specific examples or compelling data and think of clever analogies, if appropriate.

If you will be on television, heed this advice:

- Even in the comfiest chair, sit leaning slightly forward in an engaged posture. At most, the base of your spine should be touching the back of the chair, never your shoulder blades.
- Don't get distracted by anything going on behind the scenes. You will most likely see yourself peripherally on TV monitors on the floor. Avoid the temptation to sneak a peak. You should be totally focused on the interviewer to the exclusion of everything else.
- Your overall tone should convey an excitement for the value and usefulness of the information you're sharing. The audience is taking its cue from you. If you can't get pumped up over your topic, they sure won't. TV and radio have a nasty habit of flattening people out, reducing their energy and conviction. So reach for the top level of your energy output. Project what you have to say with passion. What may seem a little over the top and overly dramatic to you probably isn't, especially juxtaposed

with a professional host who knows how to turn it on when the camera's on.

- If the question lacks focus and contains a number of different questions, merely chose the one you want to answer most.
- Try to maintain good eye contact with the interviewer when you're beginning to speak. This is especially important if you are asked a challenging, overly personal, or aggressive question. Looking at the ceiling or the floor creates the appearance that you're desperately searching for something to say. There's an expression: "The answer isn't in the ceiling."
- When people are channel surfing, they are looking to stop and listen to someone warm and welcoming. Smiling can mean the difference between a viewer tuning you in and tuning you out. And even if you're not seen, smiling brings a warmer and more welcoming quality to your voice.
- Your host's eyes may wander. He may be looking down at the notes in front of him or over at a floor manager flashing time cues. Do not allow your attention to follow his. Maintain your focus on the host as if he is still paying close attention to your answers.
- Remember the Draper Principle. Listen closely to the question and be on the lookout for the verbal clue that tells you which topic the question falls under. Once you identify it, spend the extra time the host spends blathering on with her question to collect your thoughts on what point you want to make and how best to illustrate it. Then go straight into your message point whenever you're ready. Stay away from "That's a good question," "You're absolutely right," or "Exactly." Build your own independent thought on the end of the question without any overlap.
- Remember the Conviction Principle, too. Begin your answers with short declarative positive statements. Avoid expressions like, "I think" or "I hope."

If you are in the hot seat—with a reporter asking you tough questions—go slowly and use the Pasta-Sauce Principle to your advantage. The most dangerous of human instincts is to speak longer when we're on a topic that makes us feel uncomfortable. It's better to keep your answer one sentence shorter rather than let it go one sentence longer. If you feel as though you're conversationally back on your heels, make your answer short and sweet, and get out.

Keep in mind that good reporters know how to keep you talking. They know that the longer you talk, the more off-message you'll get. Don't be uncomfortable with silence in the room or over the phone after you complete your answer. Their silence should not be interpreted as an invitation to keep talking.

Don't accentuate what you *cannot* tell the reporter, the information you're withholding. Stress what you *can* tell them. Exude a willingness and eagerness to share whatever you can with the reporter even though you may be sticking to a tightly controlled script.

If you hear one particular question over and over from a print reporter, asked slightly differently each time, chances are the answer may represent the one and only quote they're looking to get to fill a hole in a story that is already written. They keep asking because you haven't framed it the way they need you to in order to fit their story. So with each subsequent asking, they are attempting to nudge you closer to framing it the way they want. Don't yield. Stick to how you want it framed.

Think of an interview more in terms of a dinner-party conversation than an interrogation in which you must answer each specific, minutely detailed question. When you get hit with a question you don't want to answer, lock on to the broader topic that's been raised within the question and speak to what you think is most critical to know within that topic. This will help you deflect any negativity or snarkiness loaded in the question. However, recognize that most journalists ask many questions that are relatively benign. Seize the opportunity to answer those directly before pivoting to your content. Deflections should be used only when absolutely necessary. Otherwise you'll sound like a smarmy politician trained to *never* answer the question. If the reporter's question seems skeptical, don't respond apologetically or defensively. Win reporters over by convincing them that your message is valid. If you get interrupted near the very end of your answer, do not yield. Finish your thought. Never give the impression that someone's questions are more vital than your answers.

THE SEVEN PRINCIPLES AT HOME

The real art of conversation is not only to say the right thing at the right place, but to leave unsaid the wrong thing at the tempting moment.

—LADY DOROTHY NEVILL

FRIENDS OFTEN E-MAIL me just before giving a toast, asking, "Hey, I'm going to say this. What do you think?" Others tell me about sticky situations they're having at home or at work, asking, "What do you think I should say?" In the following pages, you'll find the outside-the-office questions I'm asked most often, along with answers.

HOW DO I TELL A FRIEND WHAT I CHARGE FOR MY TIME?

My childhood best friend and next-door neighbor growing up, by some strange cosmic coincidence, is once again my next-door neighbor as an adult, in a completely different town in the suburbs of New York City. He is also the trusted veterinarian to our dog and cat. My wife and I try hard not to make him rue the day we moved in. Having a close friend who also provides a vital professional service can be tricky. I'm always resisting the temptation to hit his number on speed dial every time my cat coughs up a hairball.

When I think of Les, I think of someone who balances this delicate equation beautifully. He is exceedingly generous but also recognizes that he has a business to run. So he gives us the friends-and-family rate on office visits and free medications here and there. He even has made two house calls to euthanize ailing and aging pets, for which he never charged us.

But there are plenty of people who struggle to find that happy median between being helpful and getting taken advantage of. We all live in fear of a few pro bono minutes of our time quickly turning into unbillable hours, days, and weeks. Our most reasonable friends understand this, of course, which is why they say, "I'll pay you. Just tell me what you charge."

When situations like that come up, I often give the same advice I once gave to my daughter when a neighbor asked her what she charged for babysitting. My daughter loved caring for children, but like many people, she hated talking about money. In the past, she'd often responded with "Whatever you think is fair." That answer, however, rarely resulted in her being paid fairly.

"How about you tell them, 'All the other parents pay me fifteen dollars an hour'?" This eased my daughter's anxiety and awkwardness. Now she wasn't saying what she charged. She was merely saying how others compensated her. This tactic, I knew, was also more likely to result in a reasonable wage. After all, no one wants to look and feel like the cheapest person in the neighborhood. It worked flawlessly. Whenever she used these lines, her employers answered, "Oh really? That's fine."

With friends and neighbors who need your services, it's good to fill them in on what you normally charge and then let them know you're happy to extend a friends-and-family rate to them, perhaps 15 to 20 percent less. If an actual exchange of money is just too awkward, then perhaps you can let them know that you'd be happy to barter. If you're a plumber, you can replace a broken pipe for your lawyer friend in exchange for him/her looking over a contract you're about to sign. So when you get the call, try saying, "Sure,

I'd be happy to help you with that. In fact, I can think of a way we can be helpful to each other," and then suggest the exchange of services.

I'M GIVING A TOAST AT A WEDDING. WHAT SHOULD I SAY?

If you're facing this nerve-racking rite of passage and you want to emerge slightly less scathed than Kristen Wiig's character in *Bridesmaids*, I have two words of reassurance for you: cocktail hour. This may be one of the few times when it's OK to have a drink in you (notice I said one, not eight) before you get up and play toastmaster du jour. By the same token, when you get up to speak, your audience should be well lubricated and ready to laugh—*with* you and not *at* you, I hope.

Too often, it's the latter. Best-man speeches are often so notoriously bad that the humor site Funny or Die created a mock template that anyone could follow to give a terrible best-man toast. The template included starting off by saying something like, "Well, I'm giving this toast because no one else wanted to do it."

I'm sure all of us have personally experienced that cringeworthy moment. It's an attempt at humor and humility, but it actually comes off as hurtful to the groom and makes everyone uncomfortable.

A wedding should be a joyous occasion, one that leaves the bride and groom with a bouquet of beautiful memories. Too often, though, the best man's speech is a long-stemmed weed in that bouquet. A good toast should:

Include the Bride

Toasts are often lopsided, nearly all of the remarks and material focusing on the groom. The bride gets supershortchanged. This may be because the best man doesn't know the bride well, but that is no excuse. If this is the case, do some research and ask around for some stories.

Compliment the Groom

Really embarrassing stories are for the bachelor party, not the wedding. No wedding guest—especially not the parents of the bride—wants to look at that guy in a tux and think of him running through a college campus stark naked.

Envision a Happy Future

Just-kidding comments like, "I don't know what she sees in him" and "When she finds out just how much of a slob he is, she's going to regret saying 'I do'" are hurtful, not funny. You don't want to raise any specter of the marriage not working out, especially not on day one.

Funny stories are great, but not the variety that make your BFF long for the Newlywed Protection Program. Don't say anything humiliating, risqué, or that will forever alter the way guests think of the bride or groom. I'll never forget a toast I heard years ago in which the best man described how the groom, then his roommate, would emerge from the shower naked and proceed to lie on the living-room couch, leaving behind a water stain in the shape of his body. I think there was also a reference to excessive back hair.

Why do so many people give such horrible speeches? In part, because the guy giving it is inexperienced at public speaking and is too few years removed from the age when put-down humor was all the rage. Guys in their twenties mistakenly think they're emceeing a roast. They think ignoring the bride, denigrating the groom, and predicting a *War of the Roses* scenario is how it should be done.

But here's another reason: too many best men attempt to wing it. They underestimate just how much thought and preparation needs to go into the toast. Then to top it off, they don't practice nearly enough in front of other people, and when I say, "other people," I don't mean former frat-house brothers. I mean sensible adults who are equipped to raise a red flag if best men step over the line. This lack of preparation generally brings on a case of nerves that they try to self-medicate with alcohol. The alcohol essentially renders their internal edit function useless. When they stand up and start telling the first stories that come to mind, the results are often disastrous.

In three words, don't wing it. Plan what you will say ahead of time using the following template:

1. Thank the host for throwing a wonderful reception.
2. Tell one story about the groom. The story should be amusing but not tacky. It should be a poignant reflection of his broader personality, one that speaks to what he's about.
3. Tell a similar story about the bride.
4. Merge the two stories with a heartfelt or touching commonality that speaks to their compatibility instead of their differences. This disparity between the funny and heartfelt makes the touching moments even more poignant.
5. Ask everyone to toast the happy couple.

When done right, your speech should last no more than a few minutes. What I often hear most when people compliment the best man is "Wow, short and sweet. Nicely done."

Once you have what you want to say, jot down some notes, preferably on note cards. There's nothing more distracting than whipping out a crappy piece of loose-leaf paper that looks as though you wrestled it out of the jaws of your Jack Russell terrier. You also don't want to flash a piece of paper that's been folded and refolded into miniature squares. Your sweaty palms could leave that page with all the crispness of a discarded paper towel in the restroom. As I've mentioned, excess nervous energy likes to escape our bodies through our extremities (hands and feet), so holding a piece of paper may just provide irrefutable evidence of how much your hands are trembling.

The first and only time I was best man was at the wedding of Bill Cassara, one of my closest friends and colleagues from *A Current Affair*. The bride, Lisa Hewitt, is also a dear friend and colleague from the same show. Lisa is the daughter of Don Hewitt, the creator of the CBS News magazine *60 Minutes* and the former producer of the *CBS Evening News with Walter Cronkite*. The guest list was a Who's Who of TV journalism. Several of Don's star correspondents were there: Mike Wallace, Morley Safer, and Ed Bradley. Anyone working in television harbors a fantasy that one day they will produce for *60 Minutes*. I was no exception. Maybe in my case it more accurately could be described as a delusion. Going from *A Current Affair* to *60 Minutes* would have been about as feasible as Sacha Baron Cohen playing Hamlet on Broadway. Regardless, the last thing I wanted was to get up and have everyone think, "You see: I told you tabloid TV rots your brain!"

I had the benefit of being friends with both the groom and the bride, so I already had material to pull from. I ended up telling the story of their first date. Lisa had come to me a few days before, asking what she should cook for Bill. I had traveled all over the country with Bill, covering stories, so I knew what he ordered in restaurants and how he liked it prepared. I suggested tuna, and I gave her a recipe. There was only one caveat, "Do not overcook it. Make sure it's rare in the middle—not just pink but almost blue."

Bill's flight back to NYC that night was delayed, so he showed up for this first date half an hour late. It put Lisa in an almost impossible culinary situation. Even Bobby Flay would have been challenged to keep the tuna rare that night, but somehow Lisa managed to pull it off.

My punch line was, "I'm sure Lisa served a beautiful meal, but in truth, she could have burned that piece of fish to the consistency of shoe leather and it wouldn't have made any difference . . . because Bill was already besotted."

Unlike me, you might not know much about both the bride and the groom. In that case, do some work ahead of time, learning as much as you can. Interview the bridesmaids and other family members.

If you're asked to do a reading at a ceremony, always bring a back-up copy on index cards even if you're assured that the reading will be waiting at the lectern. Years ago my cousin asked me to read a series of special prayers she and her fiancé wrote together. I followed their guidance and agreed to read from the copy awaiting me at the lectern. After the first two or three, I looked up and noticed a most puzzled and perturbed expression underneath my cousin's veil. *Oh well*, I thought, *maybe she's worrying about whether she gave the band the right address for the reception.* So on I went. Prayer four was to be a personal one, mentioning the couple by name and asking for years of harmonious love and respect. It went something like, "Dear God, we pray for a lifetime of love, respect, and fidelity for Amanda and Greg. . . ." A perfectly lovely sentiment, but there was just one problem: my cousin's name is Kristin, and she was marrying a man named Ray. I was about to read a prayer for the wrong couple, probably the couple from the morning wedding. Fortunately, before I opened my mouth to start prayer four, my eyes scanned ahead to read the entire sentence, allowing me to catch the mistake. That's the moment you thank Your Maker that you came armed with the index-card backups. So I pulled them out from my inner breast pocket and proceeded. The sweet angelic smile that returned to my cousin's face reassured me I now had the right copy.

WHAT SHOULD I SAY DURING A EULOGY?

The words that you say during someone's funeral will become the stories and images that will live on long after the funeral service. That's why it's so important to make them count. Much like a best-man speech, this is not the time to show up unprepared. Think about what you plan to say ahead of time.

When coming up with material, follow the Scorsese Principle. Too often people resort to banal adjectives: "He was great" or "She was the nicest person." They leave the listeners with nothing of lasting significance. Instead think of one visual story that sums up this person's character. Choose a story that not many people know, one that reveals a glowing side to this person. Often, the most memorable details are found among the mundane happenings of our day-to-day lives.

Make sure your story is positive in nature. Now is not the time to add up the pluses and minuses as if you were Saint Peter deciding whether the virtues outweigh the sins. It's also not the time to bring up long-standing grudges or an unresolved conflict. Even if you are attending a funeral for a selfish, irascible narcissist whom no one particularly liked, try to find something kind to say. Otherwise turn down the invitation to speak. I'm not suggesting you pretend that the deceased was perfect, but don't dwell on specific negatives. Perhaps at the most you can say, "We all know that at times [person's name] could be challenging to get along with. He/she had incredibly high standards, and living up to those wasn't always easy, but . . ." and here pivot to a more lengthy exploration of that person's positive attributes.

As you decide how to tell your story, pay attention to your wording and especially to clichés. If you are at a funeral of someone who died in a traffic accident, don't say he lived in the fast lane. Trust me; I've heard it. And if there's a possibility that alcohol consumption was a factor in the person's death, don't reminisce about the nights you spent with the deceased drinking whiskey. Unfortunately, I've heard that one too.

WHAT DO I SAY TO SOMEONE WHO HAS JUST LOST A LOVED ONE?

When I was growing up, people used to say that I could have a conversation with a fire hydrant, and sometimes, even in an adult crowd, I was counted on to keep a lively conversation going. These skills came in handy with an uncle, a man I admired and adored. He was an interesting mix of gregarious and guarded—a real conversational challenge. When you arrived at his house for a holiday, you would get a big enthusiastic hello and a warm welcome. But sometimes when it came to extensive conversation, the going could get tough, with long and uncomfortable silences. I quickly discovered, though, that asking his opinion on various things was a great way to get him to open up. Simple things like, how did he like his new car, what chances did he give for the Giants to beat the Cowboys on Sunday, or what did he think of that new anchorperson on the TV station he watched. Even though I was a political junkie growing up (at thirteen, I spent the summer watching the Senate Watergate hearings), I knew never to stray into a political conversation. He was a conservative and I thought of myself as liberal, so there was nothing to be gained playing near that conversational third rail.

Of all the discussions we had over the years, one in particular remains indelible. It happened when I was fifteen, the morning after my father had died suddenly in his sleep. My uncle had arrived that morning to help my mother handle some of the funeral arrangements. An hour or so later, my uncle and I got into his car to pick up a suit of my father's from the dry cleaners. I remember thinking that my mother had picked an odd time for me to run such a mundane errand. What I didn't realize then was that this would be his burial suit.

We had barely gone two blocks when I noticed how uncomfortable my uncle seemed, understandably so.

I can't tell you what we discussed in the twenty minutes we were in the car. It wasn't a deep existential talk about our own mortality, nor was it a trivial, breezy chat about the weather. I vividly remember, however, starting the conversation and working to keep it going. On an intuitive level, I was probably doing this to distract myself. But on another level, I was working to mitigate the awkwardness and tension for my uncle's sake. Looking back on the episode years later, I realized that the cornerstone of good conversational skills is empathy. If you can crawl inside the head of the other person and tailor the conversation to align with their comfort zone, you'll likely have a good result.

My uncle, of course, was no anomaly. Many people feel uncomfortable when they are around others who are grieving, in pain, or sick. No one teaches us what to say or how to react. The idea of potentially saying the wrong thing—and thus making someone feel even worse—makes us anxious. And we put too much pressure on ourselves to bring a smile to their faces. So we fall into one of three traps:

The Let's-Compare-Pain Trap

This happens when you talk endlessly, making it all about you rather than about the person in pain. It sounds like this: "When my dog died, I felt really sad, and it was really hard for me, and I didn't think I would ever stop crying. . . ." Keep in mind that someone else's loss has little to nothing to do with losses you might have experienced in the past. Mentioning them does not create a common bond, and it doesn't display empathy either.

The Give-Me-a-Medal Trap

Our discomfort often brings up feelings of guilt, and we sometimes verbally assuage this guilt by telling the grieving person how awesome we are just for managing to show up at all. It sounds something like: "I had to cancel all of my appointments today just so I could be here. And then the traffic on the way over was a nightmare. It wasn't easy, but I wouldn't have it any other way."

The Cliché Trap

Many of the clichés designed to cheer people up actually accomplish the opposite. Consider how you would feel if you'd just lost a loved one and people around you said any of the following: It was God's will. Well, you can always have another child. At least he went peacefully.

Clumsy consoling is probably the result of osmosis, exposure to others doing it badly. Deep down, just about everyone hates to be pitied. So approaching the sick or grieving with a scrunched-up face that screams "you poor thing" isn't consoling. It's annoying and insensitive.

Instead, follow the same rules as for the eulogy and say something about what that person meant to you. Tell a story about something the person did or said that the grieving person might not know about. That's a gift they will treasure forever. Here are some phrases to start you off:

- I'll always remember how [insert person's name] used to . . .
- [Insert person's name] always made me feel so . . .
- I'll never forget the time [insert person's name] . . .

When people are grieving, they often have people talking at them all day long. They rarely get a break from all the meaningless "I'm so sorry" remarks. Remember how we discussed earlier people's tendency to talk more when they're uncomfortable? This scenario definitively proves it.

Saying less is often a lot more comforting than saying more. Your silence could be one of the best gifts you ever give someone who is grieving. This is especially true if you are comforting someone who is seriously ill. So many people are visiting and talking that just sitting, holding the person's hand, and watching a favorite TV show together can be both a comfort and a respite.

So is giving someone a conversational vacation from their emotional or physical pain. Rather than ask a million questions about their illness, talk about another topic, something that person usually loves to talk about. For instance, when I visited the same uncle years later, when he was quite ill and in the hospital, I kept the conversation focused on sports.

I'M MEETING MY FUTURE IN-LAWS FOR THE FIRST TIME. WHAT DO I SAY?

If ever there was a time to be Pitch Perfect, it's now. Short of a confirmation hearing to be a US Supreme Court justice, you will probably never be examined more closely. This performance matters a lot. Starting off poorly would be like crashing in phase one of the Tour de France. You'd have to pedal like hell for a long time just to undo the damage.

The encouraging news is this: preparing is surprisingly easy. It's a lot like a job interview or a media interview, in that the topics of conversation your fiancé's parents will steer you toward are pretty predictable:

• Your childhood
• Your parents and siblings
• Your hobbies
• Your religious and political leanings

- Your short- and long-term goals
- Your taste in music, literature, movies, and TV

And the topic on which scoring anything short of a perfect 10 is not an option:

- Your unwavering love and devotion to their child

Anything outside these parameters is probably what Sarah Palin would call a gotcha question. Realize that close-to-the-vest, mono-syllabic answers to their questions will make the conversation feel about as relaxed as two detectives interrogating a perp. Come armed with some point of view for each of the above topics as well as some kind of story that illustrates what you're trying to communicate. Needless to say, the story should be the PG-13 version. Leave all colorful expletives and provocative details in the front-hall closet the minute you arrive.

The mistake most young lovers make is that they show up for this high-stakes encounter with the flawed strategy of playing conversational rope-a-dope. Your definition of success should not be to carefully fend off a flurry of questions without getting put flat on your back on the canvas. If the questioning gets too intense or tiresome, look for an opening to show an interest in the 'rents—"So Diane tells me you're an avid chess player" or "Luke says you make a mean chicken pot pie." Without shamelessly sucking up, you're exploiting a conversational constant: other people will welcome any and all opportunities to talk about themselves. Plus, to a much subtler degree, you show that you've taken the time and shown the interest in knowing something about them in advance of the big meeting. An added bonus: your insider knowledge makes dear old Mom and Dad feel all warm and fuzzy that their child has been bragging to you about their accomplishments.

This is not the occasion to be stubborn and opinionated. Sure, you want to show some backbone and not just parrot whatever you think they want you to say. But stay away from absolutes. "I would never allow my children to go to sleepaway camp" probably won't go over big if your in-laws-to-be are already fantasizing about grandparents' visiting day. Your declaration that you would move to Canada if a certain presidential hopeful gets elected will most likely land with a thud if your fiancé's folks just stroked a big contribution check to that very candidate. Now is not the time to rigidly stake out your position on everything that could be up for discussion in the coming years. It's an audition. You want to come across charming, interested, respectful, reasonable, flexible, positive, and perhaps most important, generous toward your partner.

HOW DO I DEFLECT AN AWKWARD CONVERSATION?

My son and two daughters have taught me a lot. One big takeaway from their teen years has been how Millennials have reprioritized life's most dreaded moments. When I was their age, being ignored by someone you liked was definitely at or near the top of the dread scale. Now the unthinkable is to find yourself in a situation that's *"soo* awkward."

I'm not sure what force of nature catapulted *awkward* to such a lofty ignominious status. Perhaps it's a generation's worth of reality television that has made awkward the device of choice for creating dramatic tension in a show. Jon and Kate have an argument in front of the kids' principal at school? Awwwkward! Kim Kardashian lets the audience in on the dirty little secret that she's really not in love with her new husband before she actually tells him? Awwwkward! If you watch enough people squirm on national TV, you eventually come to the firm conclusion that "I'd rather die than to be in a situation *that* awkward!"

Despite this ever growing aversion to awkwardness, we often

find ourselves mired in conversations that make you want to dig a hole in the floor and be swallowed whole. The most awkward conversations involve a combination of two of the three loaded grenades: sex, politics, and religion.

Some years ago, our church was welcoming a fabulous new priest and saying good-bye to a lovely woman who had served as our interim priest. It was a beautiful day, and the service was outdoors overlooking the majestic Hudson River. So there I was in a small conversation cluster with our departing priest and two other parishioners when the conversation turned to the seemingly benign topic of the varying degrees of involvement among the husbands of church rectors in the life of the church. All was tame and uneventful until one male member of the parish chimed in, "Well, I would think any red-blooded male would realize that it's in his best interests [*ahem, ahem*] to be supportive of his wife. But I bet they don't cover that in the Protestant Sex Manual."

If I hadn't been standing in front of clergy, I might have been tempted to say, "WTF is your problem?" But that would have just been throwing accelerant on the fire. After a full beat of pure awkward silence, I realized what our priest needed most was a conversational first responder to rescue her from the palpable awkwardness. The trick was to act fast in order to prevent her having to acknowledge or, worse, dignify his tacky statement. So I turned and said, "By the way, what does your husband do during the week?" My turn subtly disrupted the symmetry of our conversation circle, slightly placing the offending congregant on the outside looking in. Perhaps it was divine intervention, but soon he got the message and went to get a refill of lemonade.

Turning a conversation away from the big three takes patience, skill, and timing. Here are some useful lines.

- "We're having way too enjoyable a conversation for me to go anywhere near a no-win topic like that."

- "This meal is far too delicious to risk having it go down crooked by talking politics and religion."
- "I think the world has an overabundance of political pundits as it is. I wouldn't dream of encroaching on their turf."

Sometimes a conversation is made awkward not by the big three, but rather by sexism, racism, ageism, or some other off-color remark. When that happens, call the comment into question. Here's a quick template to use:

1. Question their views with just one word: "Really?"
2. Follow up with a fact that disputes their comment. For instance, if someone just said, "You can always count on a woman to change her mind," you might say, "My wife is the most decisive person I know."
3. Tell a story that proves or illustrates your comment.

With bigotry, I feel that you can and should be more blunt. Call people on their narrow-minded statements. If you offend them, no great loss. You shouldn't be hanging with people like that anyway. To remain silent merely enables them.

HOW DO I TELL OTHERS ABOUT MY LIMITATIONS WITHOUT SOUNDING LIMITED?

The more modern medicine advances, the more labels we give people. This child has attention-deficit disorder. This adult has obsessive-compulsive disorder. And while those labels are enormously useful in helping others understand one's capabilities, they also establish preconceived notions as to how one will behave.

Whether it's you or your child who carries a label, you'll want to be up-front with people without accentuating the limitations.

Framing something the right way often determines how people perceive you, especially when it comes to our personal strengths and weaknesses.

To do so, you can use the same aspect of the Draper Principle that I teach to our clients when they don't want to answer a particular question but don't want to sound evasive either. The idea is to stay true to the conversational topic that's been raised but focus on the positive aspects surrounding that topic.

My niece, for instance, is an exceptional young woman who was born with Williams syndrome. What's Williams? you may ask. Well, you can imagine how many times in her life Olivia's been asked that question. She has been conditioned to explain it as a genetic disorder. So applying media-training principles, I chimed in, "Why don't you start by pointing out the incredible attributes that accompany Williams?" I said. "Perhaps you could say, 'It's a condition that is associated with enormous musical aptitude. In fact the musical capacity of my brain is several times larger than most people's. I can typically play a piece of music after hearing it just once. People with Williams are also extremely social and often have a wide circle of friends." Totally true, by the way. My suggestion was to lead with the attributes and then detail the challenges: "Williams also makes it hard for me to process certain things and stay organized, so I need occupational therapy to help me gain the same skills that may come naturally to other people."

Everyday-life situations like Olivia's, in which communication skills determine how people perceive you, were the impetus for writing this book. It's safe to say that fewer than 1 percent of those of you reading this will find yourself in the hot seat of a *60 Minutes* interview or giving a TED talk. But a remarkable number of the strategies I impart to my clients, who are prepping for those types of high-profile opportunities, translate beautifully to scenarios we all face regularly. The staggering number of possible Pitch-Perfect situations made it impractical for me to attempt to address them all. But if you're facing a delicate situation that I didn't highlight, I suggest you do the same thing I do: use the principles. The Seven Principles of Persuasion are universal. They can help you say it right the first time every time in every situation you could possibly encounter at home or at work.

THE SEVEN PRINCIPLES AND YOU

Everything is practice.
—Pelé

IT NEVER CEASES to amaze me how many people in so many different industries can benefit from communication coaching. I'm reminded of it several times a day, not only as I coach clients, but also away from work, as I listen to salespeople pitch us new products, customer-service reps handle requests, or family physicians explain health information. When I tell my colleagues stories of how the people I encountered sabotaged themselves through poor communication skills, we typically say, "Sounds as though he could use a coaching session."

Those who recognize what a huge asset strong communication skills can be are often the ones who enlist the help of Clarity's coaches. In the course of a four-hour session, many of them experience an epiphany, a sudden awareness of how they can achieve the results they want by communicating differently. The confidence they gain and the anxiety they shed frequently lead them to hug us at the end of the session. Being a part of their breakthrough moments makes this work incredibly rewarding. The desire to have that kind of effect on a larger scale was a big motivation for embarking on this project. I hope that, after reading it, you feel better equipped to achieve your own Pitch-Perfect transformation.

At the beginning of this book, I made a deal with you. I promised to reveal everything I've learned about communication, and I've done exactly that. I hope I managed to entertain you along the way as well.

Now it's your turn. You face Pitch-Perfect situations every day. Use them to your advantage. Put the principles into practice at the office, while socializing, and everywhere you go.

Just as I tell the clients who visit us in person, "I want to hear from you," I want you to regale me with your success stories and also to let me know the challenges that may still stand in your way. We're invested in your success, so keep us in the loop. That's the brilliance of Facebook. On our Clarity Media Group page, you can let us follow your progress. Nothing could be more rewarding for us than to know we've helped steer you toward becoming Pitch Perfect.

GLOSSARY

Best-Friend Face   The curious expression we have on our faces when we are listening to our best friend tell us a great story. It's a closed-mouth smile with the corners of the lips slightly pulled up and warm, gentle eye contact.

Binge Talking Disorder   A common syndrome that causes people to splurge on large amounts of conversation. People who suffer from BTD hog the conversations, talking and talking until everyone in the room has been put into a conversational coma.

Bitchy Resting Face   A facial expression that appears sad or angry for no reason. Despite how happy or enrapt one might feel on the inside, the face carries a scowl.

Blabbermouth-Canceling Headphones   A piece of high-tech audio headware that should signal to another person, "I'm tuning you out now, so please don't talk to me.

Busy Mouth   The involuntary and distracting mouth movements, such as lip pursing and lip licking, that people make as they shift from talking to listening.

Camouflaged Cutoff   A deliberate change in the direction of the conversation done so swiftly and smoothly that no one even realizes you just did it.

Clean Talking   Simple, straightforward speech that is devoid of filler, show-off vocabulary, and verbose sentence structure.

Curse of Knowledge   A storyteller's misguided notion that the audience knows information that only the storyteller knows. This assumption often leaves listeners in the dark as to what the storyteller is talking about.

Curse of the Intelligentsia An affliction in which a near-genius brain outruns an ungifted mouth, causing a person to start a new thought before finishing the previous one.

Egg-Timer Narcissists (ETNs) Persons who, in less time than it takes to boil an egg, always find a way to steer the conversation back to themselves.

Electric-Chair Pose When your feet are flat on the floor, your back is completely against the back of the chair, your arms become one with the armrests, and it looks like your time is up.

Jargon-Modified Words (JMWs) Words that an industry has corrupted. JMWs are so commonplace that everyone uses them, but hardly anyone truly understands them.

Verbal Backspacing Amending what one has just said by backing up and restating it a different way.

Verbal Communication Atrophy Inability to express oneself clearly and succinctly in spoken words due to lack of practice.

Verbal Fender Bender An accidental utterance that happens when the mouth rear-ends the brain.

Verbal tailgating Letting the mouth follow too close to the brain at high speeds, often leading to verbal fender benders.

Word hoarding Forming an emotional attachment to one's spoken or written material, feeling that one can't possibly shorten or trash any of it.

ABOUT THE AUTHOR

Bill McGowan, the founder and CEO of Clarity Media Group, is a two-time Emmy Award–winning correspondent who has reported more than seven hundred nationally televised stories and anchored hundreds of hours of news and information programming. During his twenty-five years in television, McGowan conducted hundreds of interviews with newsmakers, CEOs, celebrities, authors and editors, attorneys, and athletes. Specializing in hard-hitting investigative reports and feature lifestyle segments, he has worked on such notable programs as ABC News's *20/20* and CBS News's *48 Hours*. McGowan now uses that experience to coach and train on-air talent. As a media coach, McGowan trains everyone from corporate CEOs to celebrities to the average job seeker. His clients have included the executive leadership teams at Facebook, Intel, Dropbox, AirBnB, and many other technology companies. Notable individuals he has coached include the New York Giants quarterback Eli Manning, the actress Katherine Heigl, the chef Thomas Keller, the fashion critics Nina Garcia and Tim Gunn, and the singer and songwriter Kelly Clarkson. McGowan also has spoken to large corporate audiences for such companies as Condé Nast, Campbell's, Estee Lauder, Diageo, Wrigley, IKEA, Teach for America, and Time Inc.